THE
COFFEE
Entrepreneur

First published by Loowedge Publishing in 2019
P.O. Box 4178
Copacabana, Australia 2251

A Catalogue redord of this book is available from the National Library of Australia

ISBN 13 978 9 9872913 1 8 (Paperback)

ISBN 13 978 9 9872913 2 5 (Ebook)

Editor: Lauren Clarke
Cover Design: Bonnie Forsyth
Layout Design: Hazel Lam
All photography by Adrian Lander (except for page 4, 6, 8, 41, 45)

Disclaimer
The material in this publication is of general comment only and does not represent professional advice. It is not intended to provide specific guidance for particular circumstances and it should not be relied on as the basis for any decision to take action or not take action on any matter which it covers. Readers should obtain professional advice where appropriate, before making any such decision. To the maximum extent permitted by law, the author and publisher disclaim al responsibility and liability to any person, arising directly or indirectly from any person taking or not taking action based on the information in this publication.

THE COFFEE Entrepreneur

PART 2 OF AN AUSTRALIAN LIFE
BY INSTAURATOR

ALL GOOD ENTREPRENEURS SHOULD HAVE SOMETHING ELSE THEY ENJOY.

Nias, Indonesia.

FOREWORD

This book was inspired while
I was on a 'surfari' in the
Mentawais, Indonesia, after talking
to some bright young global roamers
who were interested in becoming
entrepreneurs and learning from
practical life experience. I told
them some of my business stories
and they seemed to enjoy them.
So here are a few more.

ABOUT INSTAURATOR

Instaurator was born at the height of the baby boom. He grew up in Sydney, Australia, and enjoyed an idyllic suburban childhood.

At the age of nineteen, he had a dead-end job working in a dusty warehouse and failed to gain entry into university. It was then that he decided he wanted a career that included travel, and in an industry that was relatively clean. He had no other definite business or life plan.

At age twenty-two, he stumbled into coffee roasting, and at the age of twenty-seven, he was appointed CEO of a business. Since then, he has fulfilled his vision and traveled from Down Under to countries including Papua New Guinea, Ethiopia, India, Bolivia, Brazil, Colombia, Central America, Korea, Japan, China, and regularly to New Zealand, the US, and Europe as a self-employed coffee entrepreneur.

He has built up businesses, adding hundreds of millions of dollars in equity for their owners. In 2004, he was appointed executive director of the World Barista Championship in Trieste, Italy, and a few years later, he was practically bankrupt.

He began a new start-up business called Espressology in 2008, the year of the global financial crisis, that has gone on to succeed. He is happily married to his wife of thirty-eight years and has four healthy, well-adjusted adult children.

CONTENTS

INTRODUCTION

This book is about being a coffee entrepreneur and the dawning awareness of personal spirituality in Australia.

I wrote much of this while on a two-month holiday surfing in Indonesia. It was my first sabbatical in almost twenty-four years. I was burnt out and emotionally exhausted. I was running on empty and it showed.

Even though I love arriving at our coffee factory, where I always enjoy walking around the factory floor before I go to my desk upstairs, I could see the signs that the fire in my belly that had fueled my working life for the best part of forty years was dwindling. It was not fair to my co-workers, who I sincerely brag are the best workers I have ever had the privilege to work with. And I wasn't being fair to myself. I desperately needed an extended break—a sabbatical.

An important business skill to learn is this: know yourself. Know your skills, your strengths, and your weaknesses. My old North Sydney Boys High School Latin motto is: "Vincit Qui Si Vincit" which in English means: he conquers who conquers himself. This is actually a rephrasing of a still more ancient proverb: "he who rules his own spirit is greater than he who conquers a nation." But my struggle was different. I had been battling for more than ten years to stave off bankruptcy and repay some huge debts I had accumulated in trying to remain solvent.

I knew I desperately needed some time away to recharge my batteries so I could contribute productively once again. But I couldn't see how it would be possible to afford it. It is very hard when you have so much debt that you can't afford to take time away from the business. How had I got myself into such a difficult position?

This book is not just about how to succeed in business; it is also about some of the pitfalls I have encountered and the mistakes that I have made while navigating life. Some can be avoided and some can't, but they will inevitably pop up in everyone's path in life, regardless of how successful the person may appear. Wisdom is the ability to recognize the pitfalls that we can avoid and to take action to dodge them. Hopefully this book can help you sidestep some of the unnecessary ones.

Even though I have invested the best part of the last forty years of my life working in the coffee industry, my lessons can apply to any business or aspiring entrepreneur.

Every adult human on the face of planet earth is involved in business in some way or another, whether we acknowledge it or not. From the high-flying corporate executive to the humble, hardworking mother in a third-world country, every one of us unavoidably has to make sure that we earn more money than we spend—or that we at least spend less than we earn.

What's left over is called savings. Others call this profit. It can also be referred to as capital. Either way, it's the same thing that we all have to strive for in order to get ahead and survive, whether that is as an individual, a household, a business, or a nation. As the ancient writer in the books of wisdom wrote: "Bread is made for laughter, and wine gladdens life, and money is the answer for everything." We all need it.

So once we have the good fortune to accumulate some savings after all our tenacious hard endevors, we need to make sure these savings go to work for us and earn further income. This is investing. If the savings sit around, lazy, and inactive, this is not good. Even Jesus Christ harshly condemns the servant who refuses to risk investing his one single talent so that it at least earns interest.

The alternative, if we spend more than we earn, is ultimately, inevitable poverty. Poverty is not good. To be poor in spirit is good. To be poor in spirit is to humbly recognize our tiny, vulnerable place in an infinite and powerful universe. But financial poverty is crippling for human potential. So we are all, whether we acknowledge it or not, involved in 'saving-ism', which is another rather awkward way of saying capitalism.

Capitalism has accumulated a soiled reputation and has become a seemingly dirty word. Yet the reality is that capitalism is merely savings being put to work, whether it is personal savings, or corporate, or national savings. It is worth remembering that money is not the root of all evil. A more accurate translation of the original saying that is so often misquoted is: "the love of money is the root cause of all kinds of evil."

It is our attitude to money that makes the difference. Keith Richards of The Rolling Stones fame once said something regarding money that was rather insightful: "if you pay too much attention to money, you never have enough; and if you don't pay enough attention to money, you never have enough." In other words, if we love money and are greedy, we are never satisfied and are forever greedy for more. Whereas on the other hand, if we are not good stewards of our financial resources, we won't have enough to support ourselves. These are wise words indeed from a rather unlikely source.

I remember traveling to the north coast, when I was younger, and this beautiful sub-tropical part of Australia was more dominated by hippy types than the international tourist crowd that prevails there now. It struck me that even though many of the locals outwardly professed a rejection of materialism (and don't even mention that so-called 'evil' word: capitalism), many of them also seemed very stingy and preoccupied with how they could scam money from others who had it. They were in fact largely obsessed with greed for more, even though they had little. It was rather an ugly contradiction between their words and actions.

I have known other very successful and wealthy business people who, in spite of the fact that they have accumulated considerable wealth, seemed to be less preoccupied with it, viewing money almost like a kind of scorecard in a playful game. Often they were frugal with material possessions, yet generous to those they felt inclined to help. Many successful people pay sufficient attention to their finances, but money itself is not their main motivation. It might be a passion for seeing other people grow and reach their personal potential, or it might be just indulging their own passion for an activity they love and turning it into a business.

There are of course exceptions to both these modes. Individuals can be greedy, and they can be generous and openhearted, regardless of whether they are rich or poor.

The reality is that our internal attitude to money and our savings is what determines whether we use it for good or ill. It is not just greedy capitalist corporations who are the problem. Not all corporations are bad. Corporate businesses come and go. They wax and wane. Kodak, for instance, was once a global business behemoth dominating the photographic industry with 90 percent of film sales and 85 percent of camera sales in the USA in 1976. They didn't adapt to the digital revolution in spite of inventing the digital camera in 1975 and in 2012 they filed for bankruptcy.

Apple Corporation started in a suburban garage and has become one of the largest corporations in the world, in large part due to one man's vision, passion, force of will, and intelligence. Large corporations are just small businesses that have continued using their savings (profits) to good effect. And small business start-ups are often just individuals doing the same thing.

I have had the extraordinary privilege of growing up in Australia during a time of unparalleled prosperity. I have enjoyed incredible freedom. It is a freedom that includes the opportunity to turn a simple business idea into a concrete reality. I am extremely grateful for this. Anyone can start his or her own business freely and easily here. Anyone can begin a start-up business on their own. It is only our own personal fears and inhibitions that limit us.

The freedom of being able to grow a small business is what has set apart not just Australia, but also America, Britain, and Western Europe in their respective heydays and it has now spread throughout the world. Risk-takers followed their vision and literally sailed into uncharted waters and opened up the world. Risk-takers innovated the printing of books and marketed them on a mass scale for the first time in human history; that led to the explosion of the knowledge age and the modern world of innovation as we know it today.

Britain was denigrated as a nation of humble shopkeepers and yet they took incredible risks in order to become the greatest empire the world has ever seen. In fact, it was this population of small and large business people in Britain who financed a global war against their rival superpower of the day, the French, led by Napoleon. But the French economy, in spite of having twice the population of Britain, was much more centralized and did not have the same freedom to allow entrepreneurs to prosper. In the end, it was the financial resources of the people that enabled the British government to afford to defeat the French and become the dominant global superpower of the nineteenth century. This is also one of the reasons why English is the common language of the world today.

America, the land of opportunity, has been based on this same freedom that I am grateful to have enjoyed. Benjamin Franklin, that highly amusing and intelligent self-made man and founding father, was a successful small businessman and entrepreneur who started out as a tradesman printer. He then ran his own print shop, and was noted for his frugality and common sense. Abraham Lincoln was a small businessman who failed, then tried again and succeeded in becoming arguably the greatest president of the United States, alongside President Washington himself. They were great risk-takers and endured great sacrifice in order to create and preserve the union of states that was and is America.

Abraham Lincoln and Benjamin Franklin had an enormous effect in shaping the America that we know so well, for good. They seemed to be highly intelligent and hard-working yet also down-to-earth men with great senses of humor. They displayed much that is good about the American character at its best.

In Australia, a Jewish small businessman, a civil engineer, helped shape our national character for good. He rose to be widely considered as the greatest general in the greatest war the world had ever seen up until that time: the First World War. General Sir John Monash was the only soldier to be knighted on the battlefield by an English king in almost two hundred years. This was in spite of the fact that he came from a far-flung former colony of the British empire: Australia. He had great compassion for the solders under his care and he helped to establish the tradition of ANZAC Day, which to this day is a reminder to all Australians of the extraordinary human sacrifice that is required to defend the freedom we enjoy.

The opportunity to be an entrepreneur is not just limited to first-world privileged men. Anyone, anywhere, can have a go. If a single mother in a remote third-world remote village can save up enough or get a micro-loan for a treadle sewing machine, for instance, she could start up a new business from her own home. When enough people in any population initiate their own businesses, whatever they may be, and do it honestly and excellently for long enough, it will lead to prosperity for themselves, their community, and their nation as a whole. This doesn't just apply to western countries. As the ancient proverb says: "a man who is skillful in his work will stand before kings; he will not stand before obscure men."

As the freedom to be an entrepreneur has spread around the world, even if it is limited, it has brought improvements to people's standard of living. China for instance, has freed up her citizens to be small entrepreneurs, and has become a rising economic powerhouse. The challenge for China is to allow honesty and transparency to prevail, just as we all must.

So what is an entrepreneur? It is a French word that means undertaker—in the sense of undertaking a task. "Entre" in French literally means "between" so in another sense, it is someone who sees an opportunity that lies between gaps in a market. They then take a risk, innovating and creating something out of nothing to fill that gap. This is probably a good way to think of it. Entrepreneurs are opportunists and risk-takers, offering solutions to people's needs.

Of course, there are always going to be unscrupulous 'snake-oil' salesmen; people and corporations (groups of people) who take an individual's money dishonestly, or who don't provide the promised service. There will even be those who invent pseudo-scientific sales pitches to hoodwink naïve customers into paying for unnecessary products. But these unsavory practices are not exclusive to a free enterprise capitalist society. Just ask someone honest who lived in the old Soviet Union under the communists if you want to find out how badly an alternative centrally controlled economy and society can be run.

I started writing this book waiting for a plane that was due to take me to yet another isolated surf break after surfing for two weeks in Nias and the Mentawai Islands, Indonesia. I was in the middle of two months long service vacation from my current business. This is a business I started with a young barista who came to me and said he wanted to learn how to be a coffee roaster. At the time, I was consulting to a large publicly listed company who had over a thousand retail outlets. I was forced to work for them because I had incurred crippling debts due to some mistakes I had made in a previous business. But that's a story for later on. I have made plenty of mistakes in my career, but fortunately I have also listened to that still, small inner voice and occasionally got some things right too.

My current business has grown, but it all started with one or two clients who came to me and asked me to roast coffee for them. I had a clear contract with the large corporation for whom I was consulting; it allowed me to supply my own customers and use the corporation's factory equipment. This was based on a fee-per-pack for anything I produced for my own customers. It was completely flexible and other than the flexible roasting fees, there were no overheads for our new business. So there was no downside and virtually no risk to begin with. This continued for several years, and we had some customers who came and went and some who have remained with us to this day, and still other new clients who come to us now.

In the first few years of this new enterprise, I used the money as a travel and education fund. My business partner, the young barista and I, traveled to coffee events around the world and in the process I trained him to be a coffee roaster. In fact, he became the world's most highly certified coffee roaster at one point, with the international Coffee Roasters Guild.

After about four years though, I realized that this small business that had started almost by accident, had now accumulated a number of new clients, and so I figured it was time I paid closer attention to it. Coincidentally, the relationship with the large corporation we dealt with was becoming a little scratchy. In spite of being scrupulously careful to account and pay for every kilogram of coffee we produced for ourselves, we still very accurately and efficiently managed all their coffee production as well.

But they didn't see it that way. One classic example was when their head office reckoned the labor costs in the factory we managed for them had increased substantially. The reality was we had actually reduced labor costs by 18 percent. They made the mistake of comparing it to sales rather than how much coffee we produced. They actually admitted to me that they had never been able to run a food manufacturing business successfully and now I knew one reason why.

The important lesson here is to stick to what you know, and get someone you can trust to do what you don't know for you. Even big businesses can get this wrong.

The history of coffee entrepreneurs in my homeland is a very rich one. The earliest, best-known Australian coffee entrepreneur was E.H. Harris who brought his coffee to the Australian marketplace in 1883. There have been other coffee dynasties that have been built by enterprising risk-takers, including the Andronicus family who commenced their coffee business in 1910 in Sydney; and Horace Bennett, who began his coffee, tea, and cocoa importing business in Melbourne at the end of the First World War in 1918. Interestingly enough, we still buy very good green coffee from Horace's grandson, Scott Bennett, more than one hundred years after his grandfather started the business. Being a coffee entrepreneur can in fact be a wonderful heritage for a family if it is managed and handed down well.

Of course, there were a multitude of Italian immigrants who came to Australia after World War Two who started servicing their expat Italian communities with the style of coffee that they were familiar with back home, namely: espresso coffee. Starting in major Australian cities like Melbourne, Sydney, and Adelaide, this espresso-based coffee culture gradually spread nationwide over the following five decades.

The most outstanding of these immigrant businesses was the Cantarella family whose Vittoria brand is still a dominant player throughout Australia and is now even spreading its tendrils into Asia and the USA. It was this army of wonderfully colorful, hardworking, and diligent migrant coffee entrepreneurs who transformed our Australian culture from a beer-swilling one to a café society. And this is what Australia has become: a society where all socio-economic levels, rich and poor alike, male and female, young and old, appreciate a good coffee throughout our sunburnt land.

It is this strong heritage of Australian coffee entrepreneurs that I unknowingly stepped into when I first walked into my brother's new little street-front coffee-roasting business in 376 Willoughby Road, Naremburn, in 1981. It was just a few minutes' drive from the famous Sydney Harbor Bridge and Opera House, and the main business district of Australia's largest city. I was studying psychology and history at Macquarie University, but as soon as I walked through my brother's coffee shop door, I was entranced by the wafting, intensely wonderful fresh, enticing aroma, and the exotic printed jute sacks from far-flung, seemingly mystical and exotic countries. Indeed, I was in due course, fascinated by the amazing history of coffee itself.

How was my character prepared for this moment that would result in determining the next four decades of my life?

I was very fortunate to be born in Australia as the descendent of immigrants who came seeking their fortune. My father's great-grandfather, James Forsyth, obeyed the command to "go west, young man" and journeyed from Britain to San Francisco for the famous 1849 Californian gold rush. The NFL team the San Francisco 49ers are named after this gold rush because it was a big deal. James apparently continued to literally obey the "go west" command and sailed west from California, along with many other adventurous souls, and ended up in Sydney, Australia. He then kept going west until he reached a tiny town called Sofala in the heart of a new goldfield. He gathered his share of gold there and stayed in Australia for the rest of his life. In doing so, he helped to build a community and ultimately, a new nation.

My mother's great-great-grandfather, Maurice Moses Magnus, was a different kettle of fish. He may have had the same risk-taking nature, but in a different way. He was convicted in the Old Bailey court in London on the 6th July, 1841, for stealing a handkerchief, a waistcoat, a pair of trousers, two shawls, and cash to the value of twenty sovereigns, seven shillings, three ten-pound notes, and three five-pound notes, or about $12,000 AUD in today's money. Two witnesses contradicted the police and the victim, saying that Maurice was not the person who stole the money and clothes. And that in fact, while the robbery was underway at about three p.m. that afternoon, he had been lying in bed with a woman, where he had supposedly been all day. But this was to no avail: he still had his boots on under the bedcover when he was found by the police. At the age of twenty-two, this Jewish man was duly convicted, imprisoned, and transported as a criminal to Sydney, Australia. Like a lot of convicts transported there, it seemed he turned over a new leaf after he was freed, and chose to stay Down Under for the rest of his natural life.

With these forebears, how could I not be a risk-taking entrepreneur? It no doubt took some further personal character building to shape my personality. Growing up in Australia certainly did that and it has no doubt helped to shape my destiny too.

A COFFEE
CAREER
BEGINS

The Second Part, First

I was actually still at university when I got married, and as a student, I had to find some way of earning extra income for our new little household while my wife studied midwifery and worked as a nurse at Royal North Shore Hospital. While studying, I had been working for my good friend Peter Handley in his domestic cleaning business.

With Peter's blessing, I built on the knowledge he had imparted to me while working for him. I borrowed my parents' floor polisher, bought myself a mop and bucket, and placed an advertisement for a house cleaner in the local *North Shore Times* newspaper, long before the internet was in our homes. Every week I would get one or two enquiries, and I would go and do the quotations. Using my experience with Peter, I knew how long it took to clean a house based on the number of bedrooms and bathrooms. I steadily built my little business in the two days per week I had allocated, Thursday and Friday, while on the other three days of the week, I continued my university studies and played rugby on Saturdays. Life as a newly married man was pretty good.

It got to the stage, however, where my two working days were jam-packed with clients, and I figured I actually wasn't really suited to house cleaning after all. I was a rather solidly built rugby player whose body wasn't particularly agile, and I came to the conclusion that in fact I was a bit more like the proverbial bull in a china shop. I was vacuuming the bathroom of the local rector of the St Ives Anglican

Church's house, when I pulled a tangled vacuum cleaner cord and broke a priceless Ming-like vase that had been resting on a small hall table.

At a particularly house-proud lady's home, I was instructed to clean every part of the house, including underneath every piece of furniture, which I of course had to move. The only exception in the entire home was that I was not allowed to touch two highly valuable French antique porcelain wall sconce lights that were located above the bed in the master bedroom.

One day, as I was diligently vacuum-cleaning the main bedroom, I moved the bed and bent over to clean underneath, but when I straightened and stood upright, the back of my head hit something and I looked up in horror to see the broken porcelain wall sconce light snapped in two and swinging freely from the electrical cable in the wall. Needless to say, I didn't keep this customer much longer. Thankfully the Anglican minister practiced what he preached and was more forgiving and patient with me than this lady was.

In the end though, it was pretty clear I wasn't really cut out for house cleaning. I certainly didn't have a passion for it and so I advertised my little cleaning business for sale just six months after starting it. I sold it as a going concern for $11,000 and included my parents' floor-polisher for good measure, which enabled me to finish my degree and support myself financially. Thanks, Mum and Dad, for 'lending' me your polisher.

I started working with my brother not long after this, once I had finished my university degree majoring in Australian History. By this time, I had my beautiful, newborn baby daughter.

My brother, Rob, had worked for several years roasting coffee and helping Ian Berstein to grow his burgeoning Belaroma specialty coffee business in Sydney. Rob saw a little gap in the newly emerging coffee market and figured he could do it himself and so he gave it a go. This business, Forsyth Coffee and Tea, still operates in Naremburn to this day, a few hundred yards from where it started.

He borrowed just enough to purchase a little five kilogram roaster, and one of the first wholesale customers he managed to win over was a lady who supplied specialty coffee to offices.

I could see Rob needed a hand getting new customers as there were very few walk-in retail ones. The business was located on the busy main road leading to the Sydney Harbor Bridge, and Rob couldn't survive on the handful of small wholesale clients that he had onboard.

But in those very early days, I hadn't figured out how to approach a new office manager or a café owner who were used to dealing abruptly with coffee salesmen, and so I figured I could start with hairdressers. At least I was likely to meet the decision-maker on the spot, and they would most likely want to impress their clientele and offer good quality coffee as a service that kept them ahead of their competitors. They seemed like an easier target because no one was really focusing on them and it was less intense than a café or office. I managed to get a few customers like this. As a result though, I realized that I desperately needed to learn how to sell professionally. My career began with me recognizing how little I knew about both coffee and the business of selling in general.

I knew Rob couldn't afford to pay me much so I devised a commission system that wouldn't cost the business anything. He had been selling fifty, seventy gram ground portion packs per carton. I figured I could sell a carton of forty packs for the same price to new customers, because it suited offices better given there were closer to twenty business days per month based on Monday to Friday working weeks. It was easier to put a proposition to an office manager that, if they made two jugs of filter coffee per day, a carton would last approximately one month. This enabled Rob to pay me $5 per carton commission and for him to make the same amount overall per pack. We put a sunset clause of one year on the commission; after a while, my little $5 per carton commissions added up to a reasonable amount.

When it came to coffee, I resolved that every time I was asked a question I didn't have the answer for, I would seek out this knowledge straight away. There were plenty of things I didn't know and it was uncanny how often I would be asked the same question very soon after. And, since I had diligently sought an answer, I could then reply using my newfound knowledge. And this was an important lesson: knowing an answer gives you confidence. I would constantly be surprised how soon people assumed I knew more than I really did as a result. As it happens though, that is what life itself is really like too. If we remain curious and accumulate knowledge, people will find this expertise valuable.

Lesson 1

KEEP
LEARNING

But there is always cause for humility, because no matter how much knowledge even the most intelligent human being can accumulate, it is always pitifully limited in relation to the infinite universe that we live in.

My coffee and business knowledge began to grow, albeit from a very small base. Studying history at university was not altogether helpful in this. I eventually came to realize that this academic discipline is almost diametrically opposed to the decisive clear-mindedness required to run a good business. In studying history you can hold several different conclusions in your head while not having to ever make a decision. In running a good business you have to weigh up the contending factors, decide on a course of action and make it happen, and the sooner the better in most cases. At least this mismatched way of thinking was one of the useful things I came to know about myself.

Prior to working with Rob, I had been exposed to my father's and my mother's business examples, as they scrambled to raise their six children with pretty humble incomes.

My father had a number of different careers throughout his life, including retail apprentice, soldier, women's fashion manufacturer, farmer, transport and logistics manager for a multinational corporation, and then transport and logistics manager for the Boy Scouts. Finally, he was a small retail operator, selling haberdashery and arts and crafts with my mother.

I still remember the deference with which Dad approached the seemingly impregnable and intimidating authority of the bank manager at the local St Ives branch of the Commonwealth Bank. As a youth, I must have gone with him on an occasion as he sought an extension for his bank overdraft. It was a big deal for Dad and he took great care to play his respectful part in sucking up to this seemingly unassailable dignitary.

It was in stark contrast some ten or so years later when my cousin Peter took me in with him to open a new bank account for an exciting new business venture I was to be a part of with Peter and my brother.

My brother's main customer was a lady named Val who had inherited a coffee business from a Danish gentleman. She serviced offices with freshly roasted and ground coffee, buying the seventy grams packs of vacuum-packed coffee wholesale. She also included in her offer the use of a commercial Cona drip-filter brewer free on loan. The cost of the machine was bundled up in the margin for the portion packs of coffee, and it included the delivery, service, and maintenance of the coffee machines.

The coffee was very good quality and her service was like a route system. Val would deliver twice weekly on Mondays and Wednesdays, check the coffee and filter papers in the office kitchen, replenish them, and clean and service the drip filter machine. She would handwrite an invoice on a carbon copy, professionally printed invoice with her logo on it, and hand it to the office manager for them to sign. She had a great knack of chatting to the office managers and building a good rapport with them. I took note of how she took time to build relationships with these underrated but key people in an organization and pacify any concerns they had.

It stood her in very good stead. Her roasted coffee was no doubt one of the most expensive coffees on offer in Sydney at the time, but even in tough economic downturns, the office managers came to her defense when some 'bean-counter' accountant wanted to cut costs and use cheap instant coffee instead of her delicious drip-filter brewed coffee. These same people who she built relationships with became her best advocates, cowing the stingy bean-counters into submission by pointing out that the prestige of the firm was at stake, as this coffee was served to their best clients. And if the company's management happened to be embarrassed by a discerning client receiving a bad coffee, or even worse, if one of the directors themselves was served a lousy brew, it would only be the bean-counter to blame.

Val operated this business out of her home garage, ordering some of her stock from my brother weekly and delivering it the following week. When it came time to sell her business, she offered it to my brother. Rob didn't have the capital or savings, or the collateral to go to the bank and borrow money to purchase this little part-time business, even though it was a good wholesale customer for him.

At some point, Rob talked our cousin Peter into investing in the venture. Peter had his own travel business. He would book tickets at a bulk wholesale rate from airlines, hotels, and bus companies, then put together tour packages and market them to customers at individual retail prices. In doing this, he became good friends with one of the directors of Australia's national airline, Qantas, and made sure his business relationship with this key supplier was secure. Peter was a very smart operator.

Peter got 50 percent ownership of the new separate coffee business for putting up the cash to buy it and to be a silent partner, and my brother got 50 percent and the security of wholesale supply. This seemed like a pretty fair arrangement all-round.

My cousin, however, had other ideas. He quickly approached Rob and with his agreement, offered to make me CEO and managing director at the ripe old age of twenty-seven. They offered me 10 percent equity for the privilege as a part of the deal, and that left Peter and my brother with 45 percent ownership of the company each.

I jumped at the opportunity and relished the idea of being able to run my own small business. Very soon after this, Peter sold half his stake in the business to his good friend Brian, who was the director of Qantas, so they had 22.5 percent each. I never found out the deal that they did between themselves but I guessed that Peter, being the shrewd operator that he was, got his money back from this deal and was then traveling at no risk with a lesser percentage of ownership. This is always a good way to go with any business or investment.

Immediately after I took charge of the business, Peter made an appointment with his bank manager and took me in to the head office of Westpac, who he dealt with for his travel company. Westpac is Australia's oldest bank, established in 1817. It has a far longer and even more authoritative history than the upstart, Commonwealth Bank, that my father banked with.

As soon as we were ushered into the manager's office, and before Peter even sat down, he started chiding and prodding the bank officer. He talked about how the Australian government under Treasurer Paul Keating had just deregulated the banking rules, allowing more foreign banks to compete with the big four Australian banks, including – you guessed it: Westpac.

Peter jokingly suggested to the bank officer that he might have to take his business elsewhere, as the new banks were offering good rates. He immediately had the bank officer on the back foot, and it was the bank manager who was sucking up to Peter. It would not go down well with the manager's superiors if the report came back that this valuable customer was threatening to take his business elsewhere.

This was a huge eye-opener for me. It couldn't have been more different to the experience I had gone through with my father and his suburban bank manager.

Obviously, your business has to be sufficiently large to be able to pull off this kind of effect, but the reality was that the bank needed Peter more than he needed the bank. In my father's situation, the reverse was the case; his bank manager could lord it over a small-fry customer with impunity.

Needless to say, when Peter got around to introducing me as his young cousin in charge of his new coffee business, regardless of the fact that it was actually still very small, the bank officer bent over backwards to open the new account, add me as a signatory, and supply me with a credit card for business expenses. All this was done quickly and seamlessly, with just a simple signature from me in their head office

Peter suffered from dyslexia but he more than made up for it in a way similar to Richard Branson, who also suffers from dyslexia. Because Peter had to trust people to make sure he wasn't being duped when it came to written documents, he had instinctively learned a skill critical to business and life, for that matter—the skill of sizing people up and working out whether you can trust them or not. Because he was forced to get other people to do the tasks that he couldn't do, he learnt how to evaluate character and delegate very quickly.

Looking for fresh milk Monte Carlo 2000

Lesson 2

FIGURE OUT WHO YOU CAN TRUST

Richard Branson in fact considers this one of his own most valuable business skills. He is quoted as saying: "If you have a learning disability, you become a very good delegator. Because you know what your weaknesses are and you know what your strengths are, and you make sure that you find great people to step in and deal with your weaknesses."

Peter delegated the running of a small business to me, even though I had virtually no experience. He knew instinctively that to succeed, any business needs someone who is completely focused on it, and he must've sensed that I could do this and so I was his man. In doing this though, he kept me accountable. I had to use his accountant, who had worked with him for a long time, and every month I had to go through a detailed profit/savings and loss statement.

To this day, I still enjoy the format we used back in 1986 for those reports. We had a column for the current month's results, a column for the same month's budget, and a column for the amount over or under for every item, whether it was sales or the cost of goods or expenses like a telephone or stationery etc. The next column had the financial year-to-date actual results, then the next column was the year-to-date budget, and then the year to-date over/under column.

Profit & Loss with Year to Date

Income	Actual October	Budget October	Difference October	%Sales	Actual Year To Date	Budget Year To Date	Difference Year To Date	%Sales
Food Sales	$ 16,017	$ 17,907	$ (1,890)		$ 67,779	$ 71,628	$ (3,849)	
Coffee 'Wet Sales'	$ 30,136	$ 29,575	$ 561		$ 130,922	$ 118,300	$ 12,622	
Coffee Bean Sales	$ 10,350	$ 9,729	$ 621		$ 42,439	$ 38,916	$ 3,523	
Total Income	$ 56,503	$ 57,211	$ (708)	100%	$ 241,140	$ 228,844	$ 12,296	100%
Cost of Sales								
Food Purchases	$ 5,841	$ 4,892	$ (949)		$ 24,579	$ 19,568	$ 5,011	
Coffee Purchases	$ 7,244	$ 7,541	$ 298		$ 27,372	$ 30,164	$ (2,792)	
Milk Purchases	$ 3,113	$ 2,921	$ (192)		$ 12,020	$ 11,684	$ 336	
Consumables	$ 1,963	$ 1,949	$ (14)		$ 7,968	$ 7,796	$ 172	
Total Cost of Sales	$ 18,160	$ 17,303	$ (857)	32%	$ 71,939	$ 69,212	$ 2,727	30%
Gross Profit	$ 38,343	$ 39,908	$ (1,565)	68%	$ 169,200	$ 159,632	$ 9,568	70%
Expenses								
Accounting	$ 600	$ 739	$ 139		$ 2,400	$ 2,956	$ 556	
Bank Fees	$ 74	$ 80	$ 6		$ 328	$ 320	$ (8)	
Advertising	$ 117	$ 62	$ (55)		$ 397	$ 248	$ (149)	
Cleaning	$ 118	$ 239	$ 121		$ 1,067	$ 956	$ (111)	
Donations	$ 300	$ 353	$ 53		$ 1,285	$ 1,412	$ 127	
Repairs & Maintenance	$ 732	$ 515	$ (217)		$ 3,523	$ 2,060	$ (1,463)	
Rent	$ 1,991	$ 1,969	$ (22)	4%	$ 7,964	$ 7,876	$ (88)	3%
Rubbish Removal	$ 215	$ 156	$ (59)		$ 931	$ 624	$ (307)	
Sundry Expenses	$ 245	$ 158	$ (87)		$ 1,760	$ 632	$ (1,128)	
Telephone/Internet	$ 203	$ 199	$ (4)		$ 932	$ 796	$ (136)	
Fuel	$ 121	$ 209	$ 88		$ 936	$ 836	$ (100)	
Wages	$ 23,895	$ 19,770	$ (4,125)	42%	$ 88,517	$ 79,080	$ (9,437)	37%
Stationery	$ 50	$ 160	$ 110		$ 414	$ 640	$ 226	
Total Expenses	$ 28,661	$ 24,609	$ (4,052)	51%	$ 110,454	$ 98,436	$ (12,018)	46%
Net Profit/(Loss)	$ 9,682	$ 15,299	$ (5,617)	17%	$ 58,747	$ 61,196	$ (2,449)	24%

It was like getting a progressive scorecard. Sometimes you might be over on expenses, but under on cost of sales and produce the same bottom line. It is actually fun, although it can be serious if things don't go as planned.

Wedding day with my bride and long-suffering co-coffee entrepreneur: Looloo

Lesson 3

ACCOUNTING IS GOOD

In the first year of this business, I managed to double the turnover. In the second year, I doubled it again. In the third year I doubled it yet again. That was an 800 percent growth rate in just three years. How did I do this?

When I originally took charge of my little garage business, instead of doing the deliveries myself, I hired a young hardworking mum to do the deliveries for me and I focused on sales. I actually remember thinking that I still had no real idea how to go about selling. I was innately shy and still found it too much of a challenge to even walk into a café and introduce myself, such was my aversion to rejection. This is not uncommon, and many people don't like sales for this reason.

I kept trying to learn how to sell professionally. My father-in-law gave me a few little sales training leaflets, one of which I remember said, *"Sell the sizzle not the sausage."* In other words: get people emotionally engaged with what you are offering. Involve as many of their senses as possible. For example, I would always open a vacuum pack of fresh ground coffee right in front of the prospect while I was talking. This allowed the incredibly complex and alluring aroma of freshly roasted coffee to fill the workplace for hours after I had finished talking. This unique aroma is a wonder of the natural world. It is so complex that it still can't be replicated artificially.

I purchased a set of sales training cassette tapes by an American sales trainer by the name of Tom Hopkins. I listened to those tapes continuously, and even memorized some of the motivational prompts that were designed to help sales people cope with rejection, some of which I still recall on cue to this day:

"I never see failure as failure but only as the opportunity to practice my techniques and perfect my performance."
"I never see failure as failure but only as the negative feedback I need to change course in my direction."

I also learned from another sales-training guy called Alan Pease, an Australian body language expert, who used to be an insurance salesman. In one of his books he analyzed every individual word in a sales presentation sentence and the impact each word had on the listener. This helped me train myself for phone prospecting.

To overcome my shyness, I figured I could at least make phone calls first to prearrange a sales appointment. I used to spend the afternoon making telephone calls, setting up appointments for the following day. The palms of my hands would get sweaty and I would often procrastinate, but I stuck at the task in spite of my discomfort. I found that when I walked in to meet the prospect the very next day, they would at least recall our phone conversation and it would be a much warmer interaction than if I had just walked in cold off the street. This made it easier for me to cope with meeting new people.

I learned some very valuable lessons in this process. I came to realize that most people are pretty nice if you are polite and considerate towards them. The few people who are obnoxious are inevitably people who are not that nice, and you probably didn't need to waste time with them anyway. In the end, I could almost guarantee if you gave me a list of one hundred contacts, I could make an appointment with about ninety-nine, and the one I didn't make an appointment with would most likely be because I didn't think it was worth wasting time with someone so unpleasant.

My phone patter would go along the lines of:

"Can I please speak to whoever looks after ordering coffee for your company?"

The auto-response from the busy receptionist was, "They are not in at the moment," or "They are busy at the moment." I would reply: "That's okay. Could you possibly tell me who it is that might be responsible for ordering your coffee?"

They would give me the name or if they didn't, I'd guess it was probably them and would say, "As it happens, I will be coming your way in the next day or so and was wondering if I could just pop by and leave a couple free coffee samples for you to try. Would that be okay?"

Invariably, they were curious enough to try a free sample and if they still hadn't given me a name, I would politely ask, "Can I possibly ask your name?"

They would usually give me their name and I would introduce myself and say, "Thanks (name), well, I look forward to seeing you tomorrow morning. Bye ... (name)" and hang up.

I would make about eight appointments in an afternoon and make sure they were all as near each other as possible, and then call on them the following morning while my conversation was still fresh in their minds. As soon as I saw the person I had spoken to, they almost immediately recalled our conversation and me as a result. It meant there was already some rapport and familiarity established. It enabled me to get around my inherent shyness and it was an effective exercise in getting in front of new customers.

I soon learned that getting new customers was a numbers game. Put yourself in front of enough qualified new prospects and eventually, one will want to become a customer.

Subsequently, I worked with another guy, George Greener, who had built his business up by sheer numbers of cold calling. He would simply spend a day personally delivering product lists to offices, starting at the top of an office tower and working his way down through each floor and office. He demonstrated some of the same simple, polite manners that I was using, like sensitivity to the other person's situation, and perception as to whether they were busy or under pressure. If someone showed interest, George would ask for a piece of their company's stationery like a "with compliments" slip with their business name printed on it. He would then ask for the person's name and write it down on the slip of paper he had been given, along with whatever details they may have been interested in, and then say he would be back in touch with the information they needed.

In a very quick sixty-second interaction, he collected a lot of useful information that helped him tailor his presentation to suit exactly what the prospect was interested in and needed. After doing this about a hundred times a day, I learned to overcome my shyness even more still by realizing that people are happy to talk to you if you present yourself face-to-face, in a polite and considerate way. I can now walk into pretty much anywhere and introduce myself in an appropriate way and talk to pretty much anyone. This gives you a lot of confidence in dealing with people everywhere.

I also learned that professional salesmanship is actually more a matter of being like an honest consultant rather than acting like the archetypal rude and pushy salesman. It's almost a matter of diagnosing what someone actually needs, much like a doctor might diagnose what medicine a patient requires by asking about their symptoms. Once you have figured out what's important to your client, if you have some professional solutions and you are honest about what you don't actually know, people are reassured and can be confident, and will relax and put their trust in you. It is this universal key, of putting the other person's interests first and establishing rapport, that actually builds not just business relationships but every human relationship.

It is in fact true that it is not what you know, but who you know that counts. Personal relationships based on trust are important. Good personal relationships are based on trust and honesty and on putting yourself in the other person's shoes—understanding what is important to them and what they need.

Good business relationships are exactly the same. It sounds blindingly obvious, but it is amazing how many businesses stuff this up as they offer either ordinary, horrible, or indifferent user experiences. The business that makes the customer feel highly valued by understanding their needs and wants, and structures their behavior based on this, will do well. This is the same in a marriage relationship or in any relationship for that matter. It is even true on a spiritual level. Jesus Christ said, "This is eternal life, that they know You, the only true God, and Jesus Christ whom You have sent." Eternal life is simply a relationship, knowing someone not something.

The goal though is to be always continually working at improving our relationships.

One of the things I managed to do to cement these first few new customer relationships was to really impress them with the level of prompt service they received. I realized I couldn't maintain the intimate personal contact that Val had provided on a twice-weekly basis if I was to grow the business as my partners wanted. This personal touch is extremely important to any business. It is a pragmatic matter though of tailoring it to fit the constraints of the time you can afford, and the value of the customer.

Because I initially worked out of an upstairs room in my brother's premises, just a few short minutes from Sydney's central business district, it didn't take long to drive to see my customers.

One of the first customers I got onboard was a nearby advertising company in North Sydney. I had been listening to my sales tapes that taught the principle about new customers being a numbers game, as well as being a relationship game, and that if you kept putting yourself in front of enough qualified prospects in the right way, in the end a certain percentage would become customers. I didn't really know if this was true or not until I tried it. I remember overcoming my awkward shyness and calling in on this prospect based on persistently maintaining my call-out activity, and I wound up with a prestigious advertising firm as a new customer. It was a great breakthrough for my self-confidence.

I also learned about referrals, particularly from Tom Hopkins. If someone I knew recommended that I go and talk to a prospect and they gave me a name, then the success rate of that lead becoming a customer was much higher. In fact, with my cold phone call prospecting, using for instance a Sydney commercial property news list of commercial premises that had just been leased, I would get a success ratio of about ten to one. That is for every ten people I saw face-to-face, I would, on average, gain one as a new customer. But whenever I was given the name of someone to talk to by a mutual acquaintance who knew the person, my success ratio would improve to an average of about two to one.

This again is about the potency of relationships and trust. Because the prospect has some confidence in their relationship with the person who referred you, and because it is more likely to be a timely call, the success rate is better. The power of the referral is well-known and obvious to professional salespeople, and it makes you way more efficient. I would only have to make two phone calls and two appointments per day, and I had more time for the other areas of the growing business that were demanding my attention. This is one of the classic cases of working smarter not harder. But when the referred leads dried up, there was no substitute for the hard work of 'cold lead' generating, which is always better than doing nothing.

I also learned that advertising companies back in the 1980s depended on same-day, door-to-door couriers to deliver artwork speedily for their clients' approval.

I started using these same-day couriers as my emergency backup delivery system. Occasionally an office might've used more coffee than usual and run out prior to an important company board or client meeting. The manager responsible for ordering coffee would often be so busy that they wouldn't have time to even run down to the nearest shop and buy a replacement. If got a call like this, I would simply say, "no problem," and for an extra emergency delivery fee, I would get the coffee to them that day. Once they agreed, I would immediately call the door-to-door courier, type out an invoice to enclose with the carton of coffee, race downstairs, pick up a freshly packed carton of coffee, and stick the invoice on with the address. And invariably the courier would turn up just as I was finishing getting everything ready. It would take the courier about ten minutes to drive across the Sydney Harbour Bridge and drop the carton of fresh coffee on the poor harried office manager's desk. All this was done often within about a half an hour, and way before drones.

I would often get a return phone call from the harried office manager in sheer amazement at how quickly the coffee had turned up. It would be their professional reputation at stake if there was no coffee for their company meeting.

I made them look good with my service, and the relief they felt kept them as very loyal customers. In addition, they were then more likely to refer their friends and acquaintances to me, which further increased my number of referral leads. I really loved surprising and impressing customers with this simple, quick delivery. It helped build my little business— no doubt about it! Who knows what is going to be possible with drone deliveries in the near future? You can bet there will be opportunities there somewhere.

After two years of rapid expansion, I employed my first sales employee: Scott Jones. Scott and I had grown up in the same suburb in Sydney along with hordes of other baby boomers in the bourgeoning suburbia of Australia. We had both played rugby for the same club and knew each other as a result, and he was keen to try his hand in a new business. I was so naïve that I hadn't even planned to organize a desk for Scottie, and he ended up bringing in his own school homework desk with him, still complete with a study map of the world on top. Even though it turned out Scottie wasn't necessarily cut out for sales back then, he stuck at it and was very hardworking and reliable. Scottie and I were destined to work together for another ten years or so, and we remain good friends more than thirty-five years later.

Not long after this, I negotiated to buy a small coffee-roasting business in Harbord Road, Brookvale, a suburb close to the northern beaches of Sydney. They were selling Rombouts coffee under license from Belgium. The previous owner of this operation, a guy called Tony, had purchased a small five kilogram roaster, and the main part of the business consisted of producing one-cup drip-filter coffee. This is a bit like the one-serve espresso capsule so prevalent now, except it was filter coffee. Rombouts still has a strong presence in Belgium, where it started, and in the Netherlands and the UK.

Tony was very nervy and jumpy, as if he was continually stressed about some unknown problem. As we went around his factory doing the final count of his inventory for the valuation, he became impatient, and long after we had settled everything we found some extra stock that he had missed in his haste. This was a good lesson about 'hastening slowly'. Even though this appears to be an oxymoron, even when you want to get something completed quickly, don't take shortcuts. Be diligent and work through the tedious details; it often pays off in the long run.

With the addition of this new small company, our business had doubled yet again and so that achieved the 800% growth in three years. It also enabled Scottie to move into managing the production side of the business, as we now had coffee-roasting equipment to operate and we also had to operate the only one-cup-filter filling unit in Australasia. Scott was naturally suited to production but the filter-making equipment was quite unique and rather quirky. It cut each filter paper in a circle, sealed it to the base of a plastic cylinder, dosed seven grams of ground coffee, and then cut another filter-paper circle that sealed the ground coffee inside. But the machine had an odd number of stations set up on the circular platform so that made it almost impossible to align the filter-paper when it was cut and sealed. Before long, Scottie was starting to appear a bit nervy and jumpy and stressed, somewhat like the previous owner. The problem was actually the finicky nature of the equipment. Scottie though, with his dependable, Trojan-like stoicism, somehow managed to keep the factory running while I remained focused on sales.

We had absorbed some new customers that were a new market to us. Major Australian department stores, David Jones and Myer, or Grace Bros as it was then, were selling the one-cup coffee products on their shelves, and so a new learning curve began as I had to figure out how to service and build retail sales. I must say, I didn't succeed very well with this part of the business but it did ultimately, many years later, lead to my immersion into the retail world of the barista and espresso coffee.

David Jones is one of the oldest and largest chains of upscale stores in Australia, and they were very good payers for us. We received payments within about seven days of delivering our goods. It certainly made us look upon them favorably, and we would go out of our way to make sure we filled their orders as a priority. This is a really good example of how business relationships work well. When the supplier works hard to fulfill the orders on time and the customer pays on time, there is more time spent on positive, productive and creative ideas, and less time wasted on unproductive conversations and frustrations. You become more irreplaceable. It frees people up to improve things and is a far more enjoyable lifestyle for all concerned. It's very simple and effective and is a much more satisfying way to operate.

Lesson 4

LOOK AFTER YOUR SUPPLIERS

Another example of this kind of loyalty occurred some years later, but still long before smartphone apps, when my wife and I didn't have much spare money and I couldn't afford to buy a tide watch. I used to obsess about getting myself a tide watch so I could know when the best time to go for a surf would be. As any surfer will tell you, the changing tides result in different waves. At my local break, low tide gets a bit dicey on the rocky point where I prefer to surf.

One day while my wife was walking along the beach, she noticed something half covered in the sand as a wave retreated on the shoreline. When she picked it up, she saw it was a Rip Curl tide watch. It had obviously been lost for quite a while as it had little barnacles encrusted on it and had stopped working some months before, according to its calendar, and she couldn't find anybody on the beach who knew anyone who'd lost a watch recently.

Knowing how much I was yearning for my own tide watch and without telling me, my wife sent the watch to Rip Curl, asking them if it was possible to fix it. Some weeks later, she received a parcel in the mail. Inside was the watch, newly cleaned, pressure-tested, checked, and in full working order. The enclosed letter told my wife that we could keep the watch and there was no charge for fixing it.

I was so stoked to have my own working tide watch, and so impressed that a business would do something like this for free that ever since I have only bought Rip Curl surf gear whenever I can. They have made a lot of sales from me through this act of generosity and have been more than recompensed, even though there was absolutely no guaranteed obligation.

Back in our little coffee factory, the metal die-cast that formed the plastic component of our one-cup filter was pretty old and worn, which resulted in increasingly poor quality filters. We knew we had to retool the machine. But with idealistic youthfulness, we imagined we could innovate and design a new tool that would allow the filter to also attach to the top of take-home cups as well as sit on top of the tableware or china cups. We invested a lot of time in research and development, delaying the actual upgrade of our die-cast that resulted in a longer time during which poor-quality filters were received by our customers. This did not help to engender our customers' confidence in us as the new boys supplying their product.

In addition to this, we were contacted by the Belgian consulate on behalf of Rombouts head office in Belgium. We were summoned to a meeting with a Belgian diplomat no less, who explained that we were not authorized to use their brand name on the packaging. This was fair enough, but as we had clear ownership of the equipment, old as it was, there was nothing they could do to stop us from using another name. The diplomat was rather an obtuse man who, as he talked, tried to intimidate us, as though we had committed a crime. He had a very weird habit of sticking a Post-it note on his forehead as he studied his notes. It made it a little bit difficult to take his threats too seriously. In any case, we immediately set about designing new packaging as well. Given that we were also in the middle of redesigning our logo, we had a few balls in the air.

I contacted a creative advertising acquaintance I knew at the time and organized a meeting of all our staff at my cousin Peter's office in Clarence Street, downtown Sydney. I noticed that even though I invited my cousin Peter to join in, he was not interested. We briefed the creative guy to redesign the pack.

It took us longer than it should have to decide on a logo and as we were under time pressure to redo the packaging in a hurry, we accepted a very radical change in the look and feel of the packaging. It was a disaster. Instead of a soft, light-colored photo of the product on the front, we ended up with a stark hand-drawn black and white artistic man in an armchair. It could've been Bing Crosby. It was a classic case of too much change, too late. In retrospect, all we probably needed to do was redo the artwork so it had a similar look and feel to the previous packaging and switch in our new logo and brand name for the old Rombouts branding, ensuring it looked similar but different enough to avoid the wrath of the Post-it-note-on-forehead Belgian diplomat.

It was an absolute disaster. Sales declined and our costs went up with the new design and new tooling. Eventually we stopped producing the product altogether, but not before I met with one of our small retail customers who had sold it. This customer was Audrey Brawn who ran a shop in Neutral Bay with the unlikely name of Coffee Tea Or? In spite of the name, Audrey was a very astute retailer who had previously run Cremorne Coffee and Tea and for a while had rented my brother's roaster at Naremburn before she set up her own roaster with her son, Peter Brawn, who still runs the family roasting business, Gourmet Gold.

Audrey complained, and rightly so, about the change in packaging and the perceived change of quality in our one-cup filter, and went back to using the competitor's product. Audrey ended up selling her retail shop to a retired Qantas airline employee who I also subsequently got to meet as I tried selling our failing one-cup retail coffees. As a result of this relationship, he subsequently offered to sell us his shop.

In spite of the one-cup filter setback, we were sailing along pretty well overall. I found out that the reason Peter had not come into the meeting was because he felt it was a going to be a 'talk fest', to use his words. And he was probably correct. His management style was quite hands off, which allowed me to both succeed well and fail spectacularly. But we only grow through making mistakes and learning to avoid them and also through simultaneously reinforcing and replicating our successes.

Peter and his friend and fellow director, Brian, decided that they wanted to increase the working capital of the company. We were expanding rapidly and it did seem like we needed the extra capital to maintain the pace of our growth. Peter encouraged me to make sure I had sufficient funds to maintain my share of the paid up capital. The original total was $100 and it was going to go to about $100,000. This meant I had to find about $10,000 in order to maintain my 10 percent share, which I somehow managed to do. It also meant that my brother, Rob, would need to find $45,000 in order to maintain his 45 percent share of the business.

We had a board meeting in our office at the factory in Brookvale to vote and decide on what to do. This was one of the most difficult decisions I have ever had to make in my life because I had the swing vote with my humble 10 percent. Should I do what I believed was in the best interests of the business, which as managing director you have a legal responsibility to do, or if Rob couldn't raise the money (capital/savings), should I vote to hold the business back, knowing it could be a long time before he had enough to chip in?

I ultimately decided the right thing to do was to agree to increase the capital, which resulted in Rob's share of the business, going from 45 percent to less than 1 percent. He was devastated and even though he never said anything to me directly, he must have held some pretty hard feelings towards me. He has always acted very honorably in spite of any hurt he may have felt. It takes a big-hearted person to be this generous in spirit.

This would be a very hard decision to make under any circumstances, but when it involves family it is even more emotional and exponentially more difficult. Over time as brothers, we have softened towards each other and I have since had my own ups and downs to deal with, which have been no less devastating for me. Perhaps that has helped Rob to see that stuff happens not just to him, but to all of us, or perhaps it was karma catching up with me.

Sometime later however, my brother, Peter, and his Qantas mate decided to sell out of the business, and Scott decided to buy in. So I now had a completely new business partner. Scottie was someone I described as almost 'more honest than the day is long' and as I've said, a very hardworking, reliable man.

But Scottie back then was very cautious and also pretty risk averse. Based on advice Peter had given me, Scott came on board as a co-owner on a fifty-fifty basis. The result was that we often butted heads and the business growth stalled for some years as business decisions became more protracted. I got a bit frustrated, as I am sure Scott did too, and we lost direction. We were now still supplying the office market as well as a smattering of cafés and retailers. But in business, you can't be all things to all people. In order to succeed, you have to specialize and channel your resources into identifiable areas or markets. And the inertia between us was reflected in our company direction.

For instance, in order to service our good office clients we also had to supply cups and all sorts of ancillary grocery items that office managers need to look after their staff. This meant that we had fallen into the trap of the old eighty-twenty rule. That is 80 percent of our revenue came from specialty coffee and maybe 20 percent came from all the grocery items. The trouble was that way more than 20 percent of our resources were being tied up with the bulky grocery items. They were taking up too much warehouse space, too much money, and too much time.

We came across George Greener, who had built up a distribution company that specialized in supplying all these grocery items to offices as well as distributing our competitor's roasted coffee.

George, with whom I learned how to do cold sales calls, was a business partner in this straight forward distribution business that supplied many of the same office coffee customers we were targeting. The key difference was that he supplied the full range of grocery items to the office kitchen but he wasn't a coffee specialist. His business supplied everything, including headache tablets, toilet paper, cookies, disposable cups, instant coffee, and many different brands of roasted coffee—in fact, pretty much everything human beings may need to get through their working day. But we weren't a grocery wholesaler. We had our own coffee-roasting equipment and we were actually specialty coffee roasters.

George's business was a textbook lesson in how not to handle a business. Not by George, but by the people who used to previously manage him. The original business owners employed George and four or five other drivers as their delivery guys. George and his colleagues were paid a flat fee per delivery. This handful of self-starting guys became the de-facto sales force for the company. They were all very street-smart, shrewd operators who had figured out that if you are delivering to one office in a building, it makes it a whole lot more easy and efficient to deliver to as many offices in that one building as possible. So they developed the strategy that George in turn demonstrated to me of quickly approaching any nearby prospect with products and services.

These half-dozen guys ended up being the face of the company as they delivered and got more new customers. The total business back in the 1980s was sold to a larger corporation for $100 million, not an insubstantial amount even today, three decades later. The new owners hired supposedly smart, young university business graduates to handle their new acquisition. The executives decided they were paying their delivery drivers, including George, too much. They soon told all the drivers that they could stay on as salaried employees rather than as sub-contractors, which on the surface, appeared to be a substantial saving to the new owners.

But George and his colleagues were incensed. They used to start work at four am every morning and, as the de-facto sales force, had been responsible for building up this valuable business in the first place. In their minds, they were left with no alternative once their incentive for working smartly and efficiently was removed.

They quickly decided to resign. They took with them, however, the knowledge of every customer and more importantly than that, they took the relationships that they had built up with every customer, including the ones who they had often helped in emergencies. Within a very short time, their new business prospered and the previous established and very valuable business floundered and eventually disappeared altogether. I didn't ever hear what happened to the smart, young, highly paid university graduates! Business is not just about numbers on a page, but it is also about looking after people.

Lesson 5

LOOK AFTER
YOUR STAFF

As our business grew, our warehouse space became overloaded with non-coffee items and it finally dawned on us that it didn't make sense that as specialty coffee roasters, we were spending too much of our time dealing with non-coffee grocery items. Eventually I sat down and analyzed our business. We only made about 20 percent margin for all the miscellaneous grocery items we delivered, whereas we made about 80 percent margin on our own coffee. Yet we were spending way too much time and resources on these non-coffee, grocery items.

I calculated that if we handed all our distribution over to George's company, including all our specialty coffee, it would be the same net result on our bottom line (savings/profit). We would lose some income but we could save the cost of a driver and a delivery vehicle, as well as a staff member in the warehouse. And in addition, it would free our personal time up to focus our energy on more productive activities. If we did this, we would be sacrificing our direct face-to-face contact with our customers, which is a risk for any business, as the previous business that George worked for understood to their chagrin. One major benefit was that we could focus on our 'knitting' and what I knew best, our core business: specialty coffee.

An added benefit was that we actually sold this distribution part of our business to George for a price, as it clearly contained value for him. We also offered George exclusive rights to the office market for our specialty coffee. We did the deal. I felt like a man released from prison, and our little business got a new boost.

George started out with four business partners in his business, the other partners being his fellow delivery drivers. One of them was a young guy called Paul Jackson, who as a teenager had linked up with them doing deliveries. Paul pretty soon sold out of George's business and was restlessly looking around for new opportunities. I managed to talk him into coming in as a partner into our coffee business. Paul still runs this business today as Danes Coffee and is doing a terrific job. Anyway, Paul knew George very well and trusted him, and I guess George trusted us enough to know that we would do the right thing by him. We all focused our respective businesses on doing what they were good at.

This again touches on that eternal truth: *trust*. Again, in business, as in life, it's not what you know but who you know that counts. Knowing someone and being able to trust them to do their job makes for a much more efficient and effective business. You don't have to waste precious time wondering whether they are doing their job or triple-checking to make sure they are doing it properly; you don't have to waste time on chasing up customers not paying you on time. There are a whole lot of things that just get done better and quicker, and then everyone invests their energy in more productive and enjoyable activities. At the very least, it's a much more fun way to work for sure.

I trusted my business partners sufficiently at this point to decide to take nine months off work. I had been charging for almost fourteen years by then, and as a result of a fortunate investment in the New York Futures exchange, (which I talk about in more detail in the book I wrote in 2008, The Espresso Quest https://www.espressology.com/shop), I had the resources and the opportunity to fulfill my wife's dream to take our four children out of school and drive around our big broad homeland, Australia. So in the space of a couple of months, we invested in a secondhand 4x4 Toyota LandCruiser and a camper-trailer, rented our home, and packed up our worldly belongings in a spare room in our house. I headed for a sabbatical holiday with my wife and four kids, leaving my two trusted business partners in charge of the business.

On this trip, I didn't have anything to do with the business or coffee, so when I returned nine months later, I was fully recharged and ready to go full speed again. Scott and Paul had done a good job looking after the business without me, and it had also enabled them to form their own relationship independent of me, which was a healthy thing.

Paul had a good ability to think strategically and once we had freed ourselves to focus more clearly on our own coffee again, he suggested that we needed to increase brand awareness of how good our coffee was. He had come into the business as sales director and found it hard when no one seemed to know about us outside of our office coffee clients.

Our strategy was simple. Our wholesale café customers often wouldn't make the coffee to our standards or maintain their equipment as well as we would've liked, and as a result the coffee that they served did not always taste as good as it should. The trouble was that our brand was blamed for the bad-tasting coffee. Because these customers independently owned their cafés, we couldn't force them to make coffee in the way we knew was best; we could only suggest it. In the end, it was their business not ours, even though they were using our coffee. Our brand certainly wasn't strong enough to threaten to stop supplying them as they could have easily gone to our competitors.

The plan was to get our own retail outlet and use it to showcase how good our coffee could be by controlling the quality. We figured that this way, people would be much more likely to consistently enjoy a good experience and we would get a new guaranteed retail customer. Hopefully the retail business would pay its own way and even add some savings/profit/capital to our overall business too.

This was when we bought our first retail store, Coffee Tea Or? from the ex-Qantas employee and so, like the proverbial phoenix, our new venture started from a failed one.

This shop had been run with fastidious care taken with the coffee beans. There were eighteen different single origins and blends available in glass display cabinets on the main wall as well as a couple more under-the-counter blends. The one-cup coffee filters were no longer for sale.

Originally Paul, Scott, and I suggested mutually sharing the duties for running this new retail business. We very quickly realized that this was a dumb idea and the responsibility fell to me to make it work. It was rather ironic that after fourteen years of wholesaling and trying to sell coffee to shops like this one, I was now running one myself. Most of the recent successful coffee brands in Australia over the last fifteen years or so have gone the other way and built their wholesale brand after starting with a retail outlet—brands like Toby's Estate, Campos, and Single O in Sydney, and St Ali and Seven Seeds and countless others throughout Australia, New Zealand, and the world, for that matter.

Once this deal was finalized, I dived into retailing hands-on full-time, after fourteen years of wholesaling and roasting coffee. This started my endless quest of trying to perfect the elusive mistress called espresso coffee (hence the title of my previous book) It also fired my passion for retail business.

I threw myself into this new role wholeheartedly with all of my newly refreshed energy. I really enjoyed the simplicity of retailing as opposed to wholesaling. To a large degree, good retailing is actually a matter of good hospitality. Make people feel good for having been with you in your store. If you do that, they will come back and your business will grow. It's that simple. In wholesaling by contrast, it takes a huge effort just to arrange to talk to the right person and even then, it maybe only one in ten people who might actually buy something from you.

In retail, the people come to you. They walk into your place and they pay you immediately just for tasting a cup of your coffee. I kept marveling at how easy this part was. Of course, there is much more to being a successful retailer than that, but in essence it is really simple.

My first task though, was to match the roast profiles, blends, and origins of the eighteen or so different coffee beans we had on offer. This all had to be done at once. Thankfully, after my longstanding wholesale coffee experience, I managed to achieve this without losing any customers. Ever after this, when people have come to me and asked me to match a coffee for their business, I know it can't be as hard as matching eighteen coffees in one go.

I had no retail experience to speak of other than instinct and my mother and father's example. My mother had been an artist and a fashion designer. Her parents were her example of independent successful retailers in their own day during the 1920s and 1930s in Australia. That meant she had an innate understanding of how to retail successfully.

Mum and Dad's arts, crafts, and haberdashery shop in St Ives in Sydney's upper north shore had in fact been very successful. Although I didn't work there serving customers, I remember how abundantly full it was, and how colorful and varied the items were that Mum stocked.

I set about restocking our new little retail store with lots of different coffee-making machines, colorful Dunoon coffee mugs, and anything coffee-related, making sure the coffee display hoppers were regularly cleaned,—polishing the copper spouts and removing the glass panels and cleaning them spotlessly.

I didn't have enough time to even repaint the store, so I stuck up a whole lot of colorful coffee posters over the patchy paintwork. I used to be embarrassed about the ordinary threadbare carpet on the floor until one day, a very well-coiffed, well-to-do lady walked into the shop and marveled at the colorful abundant stock and clean coffee display. She had been so enthralled with the wonderland of coffee paraphernalia that now filled the store that she hadn't even noticed the ordinary carpet.

A short while later, we did pull up the carpet and get rid of it altogether. I also re-laminated the rather worn-out main counter rather than rebuilding it, so for a very minimal investment the store looked like it had been renovated. One invaluable lesson of course is that by investing in stock that makes the store look good, you can always sell that same stock. Putting money into fitting out your store with fixtures means the money is tied up in fittings that can't be immediately resold.

Lesson 6

USE SALABLE PRODUCTS TO DECORATE YOUR STORE

The previous owner used to serve cups of coffee using a small single-group La Pavoni espresso machine. He was very meticulous but also very slow serving the customers. This was not made any quicker by the fact that the espresso machine was on the opposite side of the store to the main coffee counter which had to be very long because of the vast array of coffee beans on offer. So every time a customer asked for a cup of coffee, the owner would have to walk the full length of the counter and over to the other side of the shop, make the cup of coffee, then walk all the way back behind his long counter to ring up the transaction on the cash register.

Needless to say, this was very inefficient and wasn't viable if the business was to grow. I immediately purchased a replacement single-group machine that didn't require plumbing and placed it at the end of the long bench so it was on the same side of the shop as the main counter. Now I could easily jump from serving a customer a cup of coffee to serving a customer with coffee beans.

A few interesting business things happened. Naturally, we started selling more cups of coffee. Eventually we had to get a machine twice as big, and then another bigger one still.

I had cleared away some shelving that had previously blocked the view of the shop from the outside footpath. As soon as I did this, the sale of cups of coffee increased because passersby could now clearly see the espresso machine. Each time I purchased a bigger machine, the sales jumped up without me doing anything else. It was like the bigger the machine, the more customers felt like I was taking our coffee seriously, and word of mouth spread. Of course this can be taken to extremes but it is a basic rule of thumb: the more you invest in substantial equipment, the more people feel like you are taking your business seriously. There can obviously be lots of smoke and mirrors when it comes to this practice, but operators who are genuinely investing in continually improving their business for the right reasons reap the rewards.

Lesson 7

INVEST
IN GOOD
EQUIPMENT

Another little increase I noticed came with just the simple addition of a couple of tables and chairs outside the store on the footpath. It was pretty amazing to see how this visual signal worked on an almost subliminal level. It worked better probably than a neon billboard could have done in attracting new customers. It was almost like customers were automatically conditioned: chairs and table = coffee.

Having seen the business grow substantially with a lot of new energy invested in it, I also learned that it's not always easy to attract new customers. You have to be continually thinking of new ways of enticing them into your store.

I did a deal with a neighboring hairdressing store and supplied them with some simple coffee-makers and ground coffee at a wholesale rate. Because wholesaling was something I was so familiar with, it was completely natural to collaborate with my neighbors like this. I was constantly thinking about ways I could get more people to enjoy our coffee. Often when the hairdressers were busy, they would send customers to me while they waited. It took their customers' minds off the delay and sent new customers my way. Good relationships with neighbors are important.

Lesson 8

BE A GOOD
NEIGHBOR

Once, when I was grinding up the hairdresser's bulk order of coffee beans, a new customer came in, attracted by the sublime coffee aroma wafting down the internal corridor as well as out onto the street for passersby on both sides. She confessed to me that she had been walking past this shop for years, and yet this was the first time she had taken a few steps sideways to venture in. It struck me how much humans are in fact creatures of habit, and to get someone to change their daily habit is not always so easy at all.

Another thing I discovered was that the market leader in home espresso machine sales at the time in Australia was the German company Krups, and they had a problem. Many customers who used their machines at home returned them as faulty. It turned out that after the customer had received a new replacement machine, the technicians often found there was nothing actually wrong with the returned machine. It was almost invariably operator error, i.e. not cleaning the machine properly or not grinding and dosing the coffee accurately. In any case, the Krups importer would periodically have a warehouse sale and resell the perfectly good, returned and fully serviced machines with a reduced limited warranty because the boxes were marked and pre-used. But there was a substantial discount on them.

I would go down to the warehouse and buy as many of these machines as I could, then put an advertisement in the local newspaper, include 250 grams of free coffee, and still sell them for a couple of hundred dollars less than a brand-new one. I would make a big stack of them right in the middle of the shop so you couldn't miss them and they would sell quickly. For about $200 less than the normal brand-new price, customers could get a machine that included a manufacturer's warranty, albeit shorter than a normal one, and free coffee beans for good measure. I made more margin on these reconditioned machines than I could with brand-new ones. This was a genuine win-win-win outcome for the customers, my business, and for the supplier.

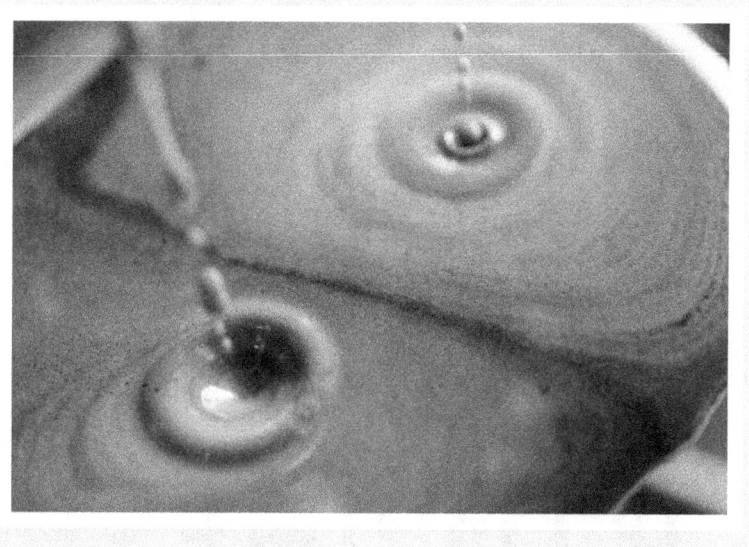

Lesson 9

LOOK FOR THE WIN-WIN-WIN OUTCOMES!

The staff I had recruited at the Neutral Bay store were a great bunch of enthusiastic kids. My first employee was a young girl whose sister had come in to sell me tickets for a charity. I bought some tickets and asked, "Do you know anyone looking for work?"

She said, "My sister has just left school and is looking for a job."

When her sister came in, I hired her on the spot. Her name was Emily Oak. Sometimes you get choices right based on gut feelings or providence, or a mix of both. This was one such occasion. I simply didn't have time to think too much about who I hired; I just needed someone and I needed them quickly, as this little business was growing and it was getting increasingly difficult to manage it on my own. Emily turned out to be a very socially intelligent person who has continued on with her own very successful coffee career now with St Ali from Melbourne, whose first roaster I helped set up in 2005. Many of the new retail staff members I hired came from the same neighboring SCEGGS Redlands school that Emily and her sister attended.

I subsequently honed my ability to hire good people, even though it is something that you never get 100 percent correct. I have made lots of false starts as well as good choices, but one thing I did learn out of necessity was how to interview and select people quickly. Because I was so rushed off my feet, I would place an advertisement for a new worker with my mobile phone number. This was long before the internet. I would be too busy to answer my phone during the day, but in the evening I would go through all the voice messages of everyone who had applied for the position. I would try and find no more than three people who I felt may be suitable and made appointments with them thirty minutes apart. If people could not be bothered to leave a polite, well-spoken voice message, I would not bother calling them back. Because a) it's rude to leave an incomprehensible message and b) if they couldn't communicate with a prospective employer effectively, then they would not be able to communicate satisfactorily with customers either, and would not be suitable for the job.

In any case, one day, the staff came to me and told me that the local government council was going to hold a street fair in a few weeks' time. The council was going to close off the street and allow traders to sell their wares all day long on a Sunday. I thought about if for a while and figured, given that I was already working such long hours, leaving home at five-thirty a.m. and not arriving back home again until seven-thirty p.m. six days a week, I would probably kill myself if I started working on Sundays as well. Not to mention the fact that I was barely seeing my wife and young family at all!

Even though the street fair was a one-off proposition and the staff said they would all look after it for me, I knew that I would no longer be able to relax on the one day of the week when I had no work to do. What if there was a machine breakdown or someone didn't show up for work? The last thing I needed was more demands on my time and depleted emotional resources, or having less quality relaxation time, limited as it was. So I thanked the staff for their enthusiasm and explained why we weren't going to open on the Sunday. I also said to my business partners that if we couldn't make this retail business work in the six existing days we had available, then it wasn't worth doing.

Lesson 10

STRUCTURE FAMILY TIME—IT'S IMPORTANT

As it turned out, in spite of not trading seven days a week, my first retail business prospered. It wasn't long before we decided to open a second store in Wahroonga, a leafy well-to-do upper north shore suburb. With this store, we persuaded a good rugby friend of mine, Paddy Ryan, to be a silent investor. Paddy put up his hard-earned cash savings/capital and we put up the coffee expertise. After having one store under my belt, I felt confident about turning this business around.

We actually bought this second retail business from a couple of old ladies who had been running the café. It had once been very successful but was now very rundown. It was a bit like the old real estate adage: buy the worst house in a good street, fix it up and you will do well.

The old shop-roasting machine had long ago been removed from this store and the décor was very tired. They were using a very small two-group espresso machine located right up the back of the shop where no one could see it. With our investor's savings/capital, I proceeded to refurbish the shop at speed. I organized for a window company to prefabricate a whole new storefront with wooden-framed windows that opened onto the street. I also arranged for a carpenter to prefabricate a new L-shaped counter and a set of eighteen coffee display cabinets to match the eighteen coffees on offer at our Neutral Bay store. I bought a brand-new three-group espresso machine to match our Neutral

Bay one and I arranged for a painter and a floor-tiler to come in on a Saturday. And over one weekend, where we lost only the Saturday's business trading, the entire store was transformed.

The key here was to make sure we didn't lose any of the meager existing cash flow so we could build on it as quickly as possible. I loved it when on the following Monday morning, the regular customers who came in were amazed at the changes and some even thought they had come into the wrong shop. Word quickly spread that something new and surprising had happened in sleepy Wahroonga. This business was on Railway Avenue in between the council car park and the train station, so a lot of commuters came past our door. And it wasn't long before we had managed to get some of them to change their daily habits and stop in for a coffee.

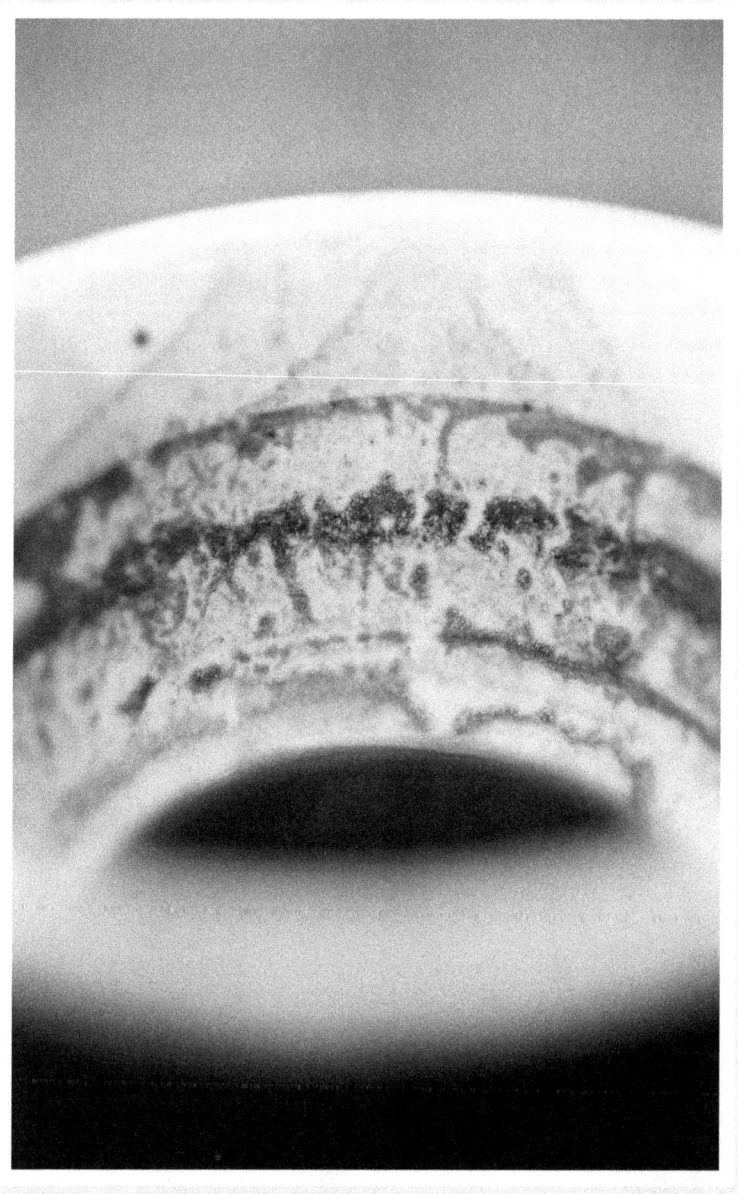

Lesson 11

CASHFLOW
IS KING

One of the best retail promotions I ever did was accomplished at this store. There were and still are two very good schools nearby, Knox and Abbotsleigh, many of whose students travel via the train station. In addition, of course, there are a large number of mums who drop off and pick up their kids by car. These two schools, among others, are the heart of the community not just in Wahroonga, but to a large extent in this part of the upper north shore of Sydney.

One day, a small and rather timid schoolgirl from Abbotsleigh came in and spoke to me about a students' project she was involved in, which entailed the students publishing their own version of a newspaper, and she asked if would I be interested in advertising in it. I said of course, but as I was now really busy with two stores I asked her to come back later and we could work something out. As it happened, I didn't get her name and a couple of weeks went by and I didn't hear anything more. I was a bit disappointed because I was keen to help the students and of course, get some exposure for our newly renovated little café.

Finally, the girl came back into the store when I was there and I very quickly devised a simple advertisement along the lines of:

'1 FREE cappuccino, hot or cold
Limit one per person
Expiry date: two weeks' time.'

The 'Cold Cappuccino' we served was made using a 'slushy' machine, a special brix mixture, which kept the ice in liquid form, and natural cold-brew coffee that I brewed up overnight in the store using a bulk toddy maker and our own private blend of coffee. It tasted deliciously sweet, smooth and rich for a cold slushy, and it was quick to serve.

I arranged to pay the very small $20 advertising fee for the student project and when the advertisement was printed and handed out to every child in the school, things went ballistic. That first afternoon after the advertisement appeared, our café was packed to overflowing with school-kids jostling for their free cold cappuccino. I even had the new store manager I was training at the time say, "This is no good. We are giving away too much," as if she almost resented the fact that she was being run off her feet.

I immediately turned to the new manager and said, "Don't ever say that again. These are all going to be our future customers if we can just make it so they enjoy the experience."

They would never become permanent ongoing customers if our staff resented the fact that school-kids were coming into the café.

I knew we had a great product when some of these kids had somehow managed to photocopy the original voucher so they could have more of the delicious iced cappuccino we were serving. There were only a few of them doing it and it amused me that they liked our coffee so much they would go to such lengths to get as many as they could before the offer expired. On top of this, the really wonderful thing for this business was that they started telling their mums to come and pick them up from the new coffee house in Wahroonga, rather than directly from school. This introduced their mums to our newly refurbished store, where they ordered hot coffees for themselves. Before long, groups of mums would arrange to meet long before school was out so they could enjoy a bit of relaxation and socialize until their kids arrived. Of course, when the kids arrived, their mums bought them something, usually a 'cold cappuccino', to keep them amused so they could go on enjoying their socializing. All in all, for a $20 advertising investment, this returned literally hundreds of thousands of dollars of new sales and added value to the business.

The issue with the manager's discomfort at the introduction of large numbers of new customers in the shop was an early warning signal that maybe she wasn't suited to the role. A couple of other warning signs began to emerge. She had a bit of a self-important attitude, and she began to get gossip with the long-standing lady who worked in the kitchen. It was almost like they were their own little clique as they seemed to exclude other staff members, and it created a negative vibe in the store. It was very hard to pin down though and I was now running between two stores and was not always there to monitor or fix the attitude.

Things came to a head when I overheard the manager bitching about a customer to other staff members, and if I could hear her, then certainly customers could hear her too. This is definitely poison for any business. I knew this particular customer had a rather challenging personality but she also happened to be the mother of one of my daughter's friends, and so she was a friend of my wife's. I knew through my wife that as a customer, she was a great advocate for our store, praising our good coffee to everyone in her extensive social network. She was, in fact, a very early specimen of the now ubiquitous 'coffee sleuth': people who roam far and wide, searching for cafés serving good coffee to suit their taste. She knew what she liked, and she knew every café within about a twenty-mile radius, including our Neutral Bay store. She was no dummy.

I knew immediately that this was a critical issue for our retail business, as customers must always be treated with respect by all staff, and that I had to act on it immediately. I told the manager we needed to have a meeting the following day. I prepared myself overnight, and even though I was flat out busy with the two stores, I was prepared to call her bluff and jump on the tools and do her job myself if she did not want to mend her ways.

The following morning, I confronted her regarding her bad-mouthing the customer in front of staff and other customers, and said it was not acceptable under any circumstances. Rather than being remorseful, she basically told me I could do things her way or she would leave. I called her bluff and said, "Okay, you can leave immediately and we will pay you all your entitlements."

She was shocked because I don't think anyone had ever stood up to her before, and she was used to getting her own way with her passive-aggressive bullying. So she walked out the door and we never saw her again. I jumped on the espresso machine and set about re-establishing a good staff culture for the future.

I implemented my newfound fast-track job interview system that I had learned at Neutral Bay. I didn't have time to waste as I was running between the two stores and the wholesale coffee roastery at Brookvale. I had to find a new manager and quickly, or these two demanding retail stores would start to suffer. I put an advertisement in the local newspaper. There was no online alternative in 1998.

I called back the three best messages left on my phone and arranged for appointments the next day. It came down to two candidates. One guy was an ex-McDonalds store manager and had quite an impressive resume and some coffee experience. The other guy, Phil, hadn't had any café management or coffee experience but he expressed a sincere interest.

I was so time-poor I was tempted to go with the first candidate because I figured it would take less time to train him and I could be free more quickly. It was a hard decision because I felt Phil would take longer to train but might end up the better long-term fix. As it happened, I had a niggling doubt about the first guy as he seemed just a little too good to be true. In the end, I bit the bullet, offered the position to Phil, and resolved to invest the next month training him.

This was one of the best lessons I learned about hiring staff as Phil turned out to be a great manager who remained loyal for many years after I left the business. In fact, he became embedded in the local community even though he had to commute a long way to get to work, and trained all the staff under him extremely well. I can only think that perhaps some of the time that I invested in Phil was passed along the line and stamped the Wahroonga store with a level of commitment and quality that endured for a long while afterwards. I also heard that the guy I had rejected got a job managing another café in a nearby suburb. Unfortunately, it was revealed that he had a drug habit and the store that was in a very good location, ended up with a horrible staff culture and was a financial disaster.

Lesson 12

GO WITH YOUR GUT FEELING ABOUT PEOPLE

Interestingly enough, the same issue regarding Sunday trading cropped up in Wahroonga too. The local government Ku-ring-gai council was going to hold a fair in the nearby commuter car park on a Sunday. The staff, just like at Neutral Bay, were all very enthusiastic and wanted only the best for the store, and suggested to me that we should stay open for it. Having drawn a line in the sand in regard to the identical issue at Neutral Bay previously, I had no hesitation in making a decision for the same reasons. I was under even more stress, handling two stores trading six days per week, as well as having the wholesale business to think about. Without wanting to discourage the staff's enthusiasm, I again explained the reasons behind my decision. This became a new way of life: working hard six days and resting one day a week. It enabled me and my family to cope with my intense business stress and yet still carry on healthily for the long haul.

Before very long, we had the opportunity to open a third retail store as a factory outlet in the front of our coffee roastery in Brookvale. We figured that even if it didn't completely pay its way, it would be a de facto showroom. I utilized a work bench that was lying around unused in the factory and pinned colorful coffee sacks to it to hide its battered industrial appearance. I then simply sanded and painted the top of the bench, got the now regulation eighteen glass coffee-display hoppers built, used an old shipping crate as a table for the espresso machine, and set up our third retail store in Brookvale.

I actually moved my desk, phone, and new computer out of our office to the back of the warehouse and set up just behind a doorway we cut in the wall between the factory and the store. Initially, we were lucky to get one or two customers a day. But as I was working nearby, the cost of wages weren't a factor because we set up a door buzzer so whenever anyone came into the store, I would drop whatever I was doing and tend to them. Eventually as the customer numbers grew, it became a real juggling act to try and work productively with the constant interruptions. Finally, we calculated that we could afford to pay for some casual staff. This store started paying its way gradually from there and again, the set-up and establishment costs were negligible so the risk was very small.

With three retail stores and a wholesale enterprise, my little business had come a long way from where it had started. In retrospect, I grew as an individual too, in spite of making many mistakes. One thing about being your own boss is that you can never go home at night and just switch off as you maybe can when working for someone else. You carry the responsibility and worry home with you. You know that customers can leave you, and your business is always vulnerable. The only security you have is the confidence that you can do whatever is necessary to ensure the business is healthy.

Many people don't feel comfortable with this kind of risk and consequent stress. After you have lived with it long enough, I guess it toughens you up a bit. But that stress always stays with you to some extent, and it is not altogether unhealthy, as it keeps you on your toes. You have to be continually thinking about others—that is, thinking about what it takes to keep others happy, namely staff and customers, and what you need to do to get new customers.

This was all in addition to the fact that I was continually trying to expand my coffee skills and knowledge. I exhausted every known avenue to educate myself. I flew to America to attend my first Specialty Coffee Association of America conference in New Orleans in 1997. I would also, from time to time, work on the roaster, and I began educating myself with espresso tasting. As soon as I would experiment with a new roast profile, I would get a barista working in the showroom out the front to make me an espresso shot and I would taste it while the profile was still fresh in my mind. In this way, I expanded my coffee-tasting knowledge beyond drip-coffee profiling, which had been my mainstay for the first decade and a half of my coffee career.

Our factory store also became the training store for staff. This was now a major focus for us to ensure that the three retail stores reflected the quality we believed our coffee deserved when it came to showcasing it. I found a video when I went to New Orleans by the leading latte art pioneer and expert at the time, a guy from Seattle called David Schomer. This served to inspire and help our baristas have something to aim for. There were only a few people in Australia who were doing this kind of latte art at the time.

At this point, there were few major coffee chains in Australia. Starbucks had yet to try their hand in the Australian market, McCafé hadn't started as yet, and Gloria Jeans had only one store in Eastgardens, Sydney. My business partner, Paul, bumped into a guy called Chris Fitzmaurice, who had worked for a small coffee chain called BBs and introduced us to the two Noels who ran a chain of patisserie stores. It turned out they were looking to improve their coffee.

Operating three company-owned retail stores was constantly demanding. Even though it gave us guaranteed customers for our wholesale business because we were supplying ourselves, it was very draining and challenging to run this number of stores excellently. Motivating staff to work and think like they were running their own business was a constant challenge. Possibly the best job I have seen done in this way was in Vancouver, Canada, when Vince Piccolo started the Caffè Artigiano coffee houses, and opened six stores, all of which were run extraordinarily well. He later sold those stores and established 49th Parallel coffee roasters with the proceeds. Vince is a very dedicated and smart coffee entrepreneur.

As I found out from my subsequent exposure to the franchise industry, cold statistics bear out the fact that an owner-operator almost always improves the profitability and therefore reliability of a store, versus a store run under company management.

One of the key lessons I learned during this time, thanks to a Brad Sugars sales seminar I attended with my old friend Peter Handley, was the power of a free offer. It applies not just to retail but any business. There are some basic common-sense principles though. I started offering coffee 'club' cards at our first store at Neutral Bay really aggressively to try and combat a competitor a few doors down. Initially, we offered every fifth coffee for free. This was probably a bit over the top and we subsequently changed it to every eighth coffee for free.

Down the track, I also implemented a quarterly prize, like a coffee machine or something substantial that motivated customers to hand in their completed card with their name, phone number, and email address on it. This of course is the beginning of a customer database, which can be invaluable for marketing and building a business.

In addition to this, I ordered business-size cards that simply had 'one free coffee' printed on them. I used to always carry a few around with me in my wallet, and whenever a random conversation sprang up which ended on the topic of coffee, I would just give the person I was speaking with a card on the spot. It would sometimes be when I was at the bank or on the road, but this little generous, no-strings-attached gesture never failed to attract goodwill.

Invariably, a high percentage of people who received them would end up coming into the store at some point to get their free coffee. Once they did this, they were offered a coffee club card, so they could go on receiving a regular free coffee. They would almost always take the club card as they were already in the process of receiving a free one anyway. This became a measuring tool for promotions.

At the end of the month, if there were different promotions, the club card would be pre-marked with a symbol so we knew whether they were a new customer and which promotion had brought them into the shop. The idea here was to simply get a percentage of new people through the doors to try our product for the first time. The product stood up on its own merits, and so a certain percentage became new long-term customers.

If you implement this technique, once you have these new long-term customers, you can calculate roughly how long a customer stays with you and how often they order. Once you calculate this, you know the average lifelong value of a customer.

This is really helpful in any business. If you know the value of a customer to your business, then the next thing you need to do is figure out how much it costs to attract a new customer. As long as it is less than the value of the customer, you will save some money. The less it costs to gain a new customer, the more savings (profit) you will accumulate.

One important key in validating this is accurate measuring. If you invest in advertising to attract new customers, it is critical to be able to measure how many new customers you gain as a result so you can do this calculation for your business. This is the same for all businesses small, medium, and large. And this is what the humble free coffee card can do. It is this simple, basic business and marketing approach that subsequently turned my whole life around in a rather miraculous way, which I'll get into later.

At this point in 1999, our little Danbrew coffee business, or Danes, as it is now known, was flying along with three retail stores and a wholesale roastery.

But in the midst of this, I made a huge mistake. While working such long hours and with such little family time at home, I succumbed to an infatuation. I had a young eighteen-year-old attractive staff member working for me. While she had no particular interest in her forty-year-old boss, I let my mind pay too much attention to her. I wrote what I thought was a poetic letter explaining why I could never have anything to do with her romantically, which came as a shock to her because of course she had never entertained such a preposterous idea in the first place. While nothing untoward actually happened, it was very awkward for her.

I had also caused serious hurt to my long-suffering beautiful wife, and I was horrified that I could cause so much pain. I would have been scathing if I had found someone else causing such drama, and yet here, I found myself the culprit.

As a result, we made changes in the business. We appointed our office manager, a senior lady, to implement a program to make all our staff feel safe. And I immediately wrote a letter to all the young staff working in our stores, clarifying what I had done wrong and reassuring them of their safety and the procedures available to them.

My business partner was a long-suffering co-worker during all this. It was not long afterwards when he was in the nearby Campbell's Cash and Carry store, trying to purchase some last-minute small items for a customer, that he came across Chris Fitzmaurice. Chris told him that the patisserie chain he worked for was putting their coffee supply out to tender, and he encouraged us to put our hat in the ring. As sales director, Paul focused on trying to win this sizeable new customer.

As Paul talked to the patisserie owners, we discovered that they were on the lookout for not just a new coffee supplier, but a new coffee business partnership. We figured it could be a really good fit if we could supply coffee to their stores and if they helped us gain franchising expertise for our fledging chain of cafés. I clearly remember meeting up with the two founders at our Neutral Bay store. Our Neutral Bay retail property was in a unique precinct. The individual properties were all owned on a strata basis in the same way that most Australian home apartments are legally set up. This sounded good in theory but in practice, what was actually happening was that a property developer was buying up the retail properties one by one, and then leaving them vacant to try and drive out the other retailers so the developer could take over the entire building and redevelop it. This meant that there was an increasing number of vacant shops around us.

The irony was that our little coffee house was booming. When the patisserie owners came to meet me, we all sat at a table looking down an almost completely abandoned shopping mall corridor. They could also look into our shop through the large glass window and see something that was quite astounding from a retail point of view, and also a bit of a harbinger of the national coffee culture to come. The counter was surrounded by a throng of people several deep, all seeking their favorite coffee. The two patisserie owners, who had about seventy franchise stores across four states at that stage, kept on looking again and again down the abandoned shopping mall corridor and back to our crowded little store. They finally said, "We don't know what you are doing here, but we need this coffee culture replicated in our stores."

As negotiations proceeded, it became clear that they were not really interested in helping us build a chain of specialty coffee stores, but they were more interested in fixing their own coffee. In the end, Paul decided this wasn't for him. So I had to weigh up whether I should leave the relatively safe little suburban business that I had grown from a garage-run start-up, still with room to grow, or jump ship and join with two guys I didn't know that well and take on a business challenge that was more national in scale.

It was a very hard decision. One path was the safe, comfortable, and familiar world I had been used to, and the other was very challenging and completely unknown territory. I wavered back and forth in my mind, weighing up the pros and cons of the alternatives.

In the meantime, the patisserie chain owners had wisely set up a coffee committee from among their franchisees. The committee members were concerned and committed leading coffee operators who were involved in making the decision about whose coffee they would use for the whole chain. There were about twelve young-gun coffee entrepreneurs at the time who came down to our factory in Harbord Road, Brookvale, and we made our presentation. We then had to design a blend with their input that straddled the three main coffee brands that they were using at the time: Vittoria, Lavazza, and Illy Caffé. This took numerous variations as we rigorously pursued the best possible outcome.

We succeeded in coming up with a blend that we felt met the brief, and went to trial it with the coffee committee members at their chosen store in Marrickville which was run by one of those smart young coffee entrepreneurs by the name of Chris Mavris, now of Soul Origin fame. Thankfully, these brash young coffee entrepreneurs accepted the blend we had developed for them.

And finally, I sold my shares to Paul. I felt a bit like how Abraham of old may have felt when he offered to take the more difficult unknown mountainous path and allow his relative Lot to choose the easy flat road across the plains. I was given 20 percent ownership of the new start-up business and a loan to the business of $150,000 from the patisserie owners as start-up capital. I set about establishing a totally new coffee venture that included a brand-new coffee-roasting production and training facility.

One store-owner, George from Burwood, immediately gave me a really hard time in our first meeting, aggressively saying that he knew who Vittoria was, Australia's leading coffee brand, and he knew who Lavazza was, Italy's leading coffee brand, but he didn't know who I was. He asked pointedly, "Why should I risk my hard-earned coffee business with someone I have never heard of before?"

I calmly listened to him and I guess instinctively put myself in his shoes, as if I were in my own store. I then responded by steadily saying, "I am not here to preserve your business as it is now, George. I'm here to help you increase your business from what it is now to 25 percent more, 50 percent more, or even double if I can."

It quieted him down, and since he was one of the leading, more assertive personalities, most of the others went along and were willing to give me a fair go.

One of the attributes that I think helped me in winning over the other initial seventy or so store-owners was that I had actually been a barista myself, and I'd had to manage three of my own retail stores. So when they came up with objections like "I don't have time to do all this fussing around to make a good coffee," I would simply say, "You don't have time not to."

Not only that, but I could give them concrete examples of how dedication to good coffee quality results in better business. Without exception, everyone who pays attention to the good quality of the coffee they serve their customers, even to the point of redoing a coffee if it is not good enough, will win in the long run because customers like business people who take good care of them. At the end of the day, a café is a hospitality business. If you make people feel good, they will come back again and again. Of course, if you repeatedly take too long to serve them, you can lose your customers' confidence, so that won't work either. It is a balancing act between taking care, fixing problems, and being professionally quick. It is a formula that works everywhere in every business. It can actually be almost unspoken as a good chef or good barista focuses passionately on their task. But speed and quality are surefire winners. That is what experience, dedication, and passion bring to the surface. It is very engaging.

One of the smartest ideas the franchisors had implemented was to establish the store-owners so that the coffee companies did not own and lend the machines to them as café operators. This made the changeover much easier as all the store-owners owned their own coffee machines and could easily change suppliers if they chose to. Once a coffee company supplies the equipment, even though it seems enticing to the new coffee entrepreneur because they don't have to pay thousands of dollars for the equipment upfront, it can become a big trap. The cost of the machine is of course factored into the coffee price over the long term, so you end up paying for it anyway, but it means you have less leverage when it comes to demanding quality and service. Once the machine is installed, the coffee company doesn't have to work so hard to keep you.

In my case, I had to pull out every stop to ensure the coffee and service was as good as it could possibly be because the only way I could try and keep them as a customer would be with my good performance. This dynamic puts more emphasis on keeping the coffee supplier on their toes, and I was comfortable with this by now after almost twenty years of both wholesaling and retailing coffee.

At the same time as winning over the store-owners one by one, I set about establishing the brand-new coffee roasting plant. As it happened, I used to receive faxes from a guy in London who sold second-hand coffee machinery. (Yes, people were still using fax-machines in 1999). Coincidentally, at the same time as I was needing to set up this new coffee factory, I received a fax about a secondhand sixty kilogram Probat coffee roaster for sale for about $23,000. That was very cheap even back then. We had been roasting on a forty-five kilogram Probat previously, and I liked the feel of the old-school solid quality German engineering. Probat has been manufacturing coffee roasters since before the automobile was invented. They started in fact in 1868, and they are still the world's leading roaster manufacturer to this day. I have visited their factory in Emmerich, Germany, and they do have an incredible culture of excellence that has sustained them over a very long period of time.

I immediately ordered and paid for the secondhand Probat roaster and eagerly inspected the shipping container when it finally arrived some months later on the docks at Port Botany, Sydney. As the container was opened, I saw everything was as it should be, with the lovely brass analogue temperature exhaust gauge and the cast-iron ballast door-opening arm in perfect order.

Unfortunately, even though it had been shipped halfway around the world safely, somewhere in between being loaded onto a truck at the port and being driven forty-five minutes to my factory, the roaster had tipped over inside the container and broken its restraints. The lovely brass gauge was dented, the glass was broken, and the rustic cast-iron arm had been snapped in two.

I engaged a burner specialist, who was a real rough diamond tradie by the name of Ross, to help me install it. Ross was one of those unqualified yet highly intelligent tradesman who can instinctively understand and solve problems. When I enquired about obtaining the original equipment schematics from Probat, with typical German thoroughness, they informed me that the roaster had actually been manufactured in about 1956 but it had been installed and modified in Ireland, by a well-known Irish coffee company called Bewleys. And as a result, they would not release the machine diagrams to me because they would not match the modifications that had been carried out.

With no diagrams to follow, Ross and I managed to piece together the broken items and reconnect the de-stoner, and install new after-burners. Ross recommended the latest natural-gas burner from the UK, and he installed it and we first fired it up in early March, 2000. This roaster turned out to be an amazing piece of equipment. Over the following decade and a half, it produced an enormous amount of high-quality coffee that enhanced the lives of thousands of ordinary people. What I didn't know at the time was that this type of roaster was pretty rare and created a unique means of transferring heat to coffee beans that is ideally suited to espresso coffee—and espresso coffee was what I had to now focus on exclusively.

This new business was indeed 100 percent espresso based, whereas with my previous business, the majority of my time had been invested in drip-filter coffee. The demand for espresso-based coffee in Australia had changed enormously and I adapted the business operations to these new changes. In some ways, it made my job as a coffee roaster much simpler. I had one blend to worry about, not including decaffeinated coffee, whereas previously I had to worry about thirty or more different single origins and blends for not just espresso and drip-filter but French press as well. This was almost *mission impossible* for one person to manage properly as well as managing three retail outlets.

At the same time, I relished the idea of democratizing good coffee taste. The goal I set myself was to create the best possible quality coffee, to as wide an audience as possible, in as many stores as possible—to make good-tasting coffee the rule not the exception, so that when someone went to their local nearby café, they expected to be delighted rather than disappointed. Back in the late 1990s, one of the biggest problems was to just train operators to keep their equipment clean and their grinder blades sharp. My wife would often say, "Too many coffees taste as if they've been made with milk in a dirty ashtray." This is because coffee oils very quickly leave a coating on the equipment and turn rancid, and make even the best coffee taste ashy and dirty.

One thing I had noticed previously, in our Neutral Bay store in particular, was that there were no demographic barriers for Australians who liked and sought out good-tasting coffee. Apart from my wife's middle-aged school-mum friend in Wahroonga, we had truck delivery drivers, taxi drivers, young gym junkies, radio advertising executives, secretaries, university students, and well-traveled successful men and women of the world who all sought out our store for the same reason: the specialty coffee taste was good and we were seeking as hard and as excellently as we could to deliver it to their palates.

In my new expanded yet focused role, I very quickly discovered how the emerging Australian consumer preference for good coffee extended even more profoundly across all demographics. There was one leading coffee store-owner who had been on the coffee committee when I started with this new business. He was in Mt Druitt of all places, which had a rather a notorious reputation in Sydney's western suburbs. I was so impressed when I went there as the store-owner had won over the local community and captured the hearts of lots of customers, partly because he was already doing latte art to rival the best in the world and the locals loved it. Forever afterwards, whenever someone told me how tough it might have been to build their coffee business in their local area, I knew if it could be achieved in Mt Druitt, it could be done anywhere. I am still uncovering the extent of this reality.

Someone once said the most valuable worker is the one who can make problems go away quickly. This is something that only happens with diligence and strategic thinking. One example that springs to mind in regard to this occurred at about the same time as I was setting up my new coffee factory when the 2000 Olympic ticketing floundered into chaos. The NSW state government established the Sydney Olympic Organizing committee, who had in turn contracted someone to organize ticketing. But problems emerged with pricing and availability. It became a large political problem leading into the Sydney Olympics in 2000, because the organizing committee was politically appointed and so the government was getting blamed for the problem.

After a media furor over the 'ticketing fiasco,' it seemed to very quickly go away. Subsequently, the Sydney Olympic games sold 6.7 million tickets, a record sale of more than 92.4 percent of the available tickets. Some years later, I met the man who the government employed, at a rather exorbitant rate, to fix their problem. It turned out the tickets were being printed in America and there had been a communication problem with the printing company. This guy realized that it was no good talking from so far away, so as soon as he had diagnosed the source of the problem, he jumped on a plane and flew to America to sort it out out face-to-face on the spot. A pretty simple solution on the surface, but he was a very strategic and quick-thinking entrepreneur who was subsequently rehired at a very good rate many times over to solve different problems for lots of other operations.

On a much simpler scale, I faced my own challenges. One Friday afternoon as I began my one-and-a-half-hour commute home after a very busy week, I received a call on my mobile cell phone from the store in Birkenhead near the inner city. They were complaining about the quality and taste of the new coffee. I immediately turned around, and in spite of my fatigue, drove straight to the store. As I arrived, I noticed a lot of major building works underway in and around the shopping precinct.

Once I got to the store, I naturally slipped into my diagnostic, consultative sales mode that I had learned from wholesaling, perhaps similar to how a doctor may adopt their professional demeanor, and tried to understand what was going on. I made a few coffees on the machine, and checked for signs of equipment problems and cleanliness that might affect taste, but found nothing. Finally, I made a coffee that I was confident tasted okay and gave it to the store-owner to taste. He agreed it was fine. He then made some coffees himself and we both agreed there was no problem now. I suggested that a possible cause of the problem could have been that the building works temporarily affected the water quality as I had seen the construction guys working on water pipes on my way in. In any case, I finally left for home much later than normal, but we were both satisfied that there was nothing wrong with the coffee.

It is vital when any problem like this emerges to snuff it out as quickly as possible. Otherwise, other people's perceptions will be affected and the way they feel about their previously problem-free coffee can very quickly be adversely affected. People are about twice as likely to tell others about their complaints in comparison to their compliments. On top of this, the process of tasting is an incredibly complex human experience. Perceptions play an enormous part in the way we experience what we taste, whether we know it or not. If they taste anything with a negative thought in mind, it will be very hard to convince them it tastes ok. This makes it even more important to deal with complaints quickly.

As it happened, the first thing after the weekend on the following Monday morning, I had a regular monthly management meeting with my new business partners. One of them was a pastry chef and he seemed keen to shake me up a bit. Right at the start of the meeting, he challenged me by saying there were problems with the coffee. I calmly asked him exactly what the problems were. It finally boiled down to one problem, not multiple 'problems', and that was at Birkenhead. I confirmed with him that there were no other stores with any problems and went on to explain that I had called into Birkenhead on the previous Friday evening and made coffee with the store-owner, who had agreed that the coffee was actually fine, and the issue may well have been a result of dirty water from the extensive earth-moving and building going on around his shopping area.

It appeared that the complaint had been recorded at head office but because I had been on the spot at such an unlikely late hour on the Friday, the fact that I had already solved the problem had not been reported. The negativity disappeared immediately and most importantly, there was no need for anyone to feel nervous about the new coffee. This kind of confidence is essential to building trust in quality. Confidence shapes people's perceptions and it is a fact that our perceptions clearly affect how we taste food and coffee.

Tasting coffee, or wine for that matter, is in fact an extremely subjective process. Normally when tasting coffee professionally, it should be done in a laboratory environment with plain walls to avoid visual stimuli, and there should be no noise or talking to avoid aural stimuli. Even then it is very problematic to get consistent taste results between people as flavor can vary according to temperature, and our palates can also be affected by what we have previously tasted. Even being a professional taster applies to how we perceive taste.

There are a number of studies that highlight the influences on how we perceive what we taste.

One test involved playing different music in a wine shop. There were three types: the first one was French accordion music, synonymous with French culture; the second was Andean pipe tunes synonymous with Chile; the third was a didgeridoo that is obviously unique to Australia. At different stages throughout the day, the different music was played exclusively, and the sales of the relevant country's wines were monitored. As it happened, whenever a particular type of music was being played, sales of that country's wines skyrocketed significantly. The wine buyers were asked as they exited if the music playing in the store had affected their wine purchase in any way. They immediately denied that this could have been the case because they prided themselves on their wine knowledge and their ability to choose wines based on their extensive expertise. So influencing people's perceptions is relatively easy, but getting them to be honest about it is another thing altogether.

Another wine-tasting experiment involving music has been conducted with five wines being tasted. There was different music playing for all five wines. Without the subjects knowing, a control sample was included, so wine number one and wine number four were identical. For wine number one, the music that played was meditative water-lily piano music that is extremely gentle and restful.

For wine number four, the music was Wagner's "Ride Of The Valkyries," which is extremely dramatic and stirring. Every one of the participants tasted and scored the identical wine sample completely differently to the control sample. In this case, when they were interviewed and asked if the music playing had affected their ability to taste the wines, they immediately blamed the music for their inability to recognize the two identical wines, presumably because their pride would not allow them to admit that they were not otherwise capable of tasting objectively.

A further experiment that serves to show how difficult it is to actually be objective when tasting was conducted with experienced professional wine-tasters versus novices. When a particular varietal was announced—say, Syrah—in spite of the fact that it might have actually been Merlot, all the professional tasters evaluated the wine based on their predisposed knowledge of what a Syrah would taste like. The novices, who had no idea what a Syrah was and had no preconceptions or biases, were often more accurate in their analysis of the wine. So the more we know about a particular wine or coffee, the more biased we can potentially be!

All these lessons apply equally to coffee. Coffee is actually much more complex than wine and has possibly three times as many aromatic compounds. Many of these may be fleeting, so a cup of coffee can often change as it cools and flavors that were apparent to one taster will be different for someone else tasting the identical cup at a later stage.

Knowing all this about a very narrow range of stimuli, and given all the built-in predispositions we carry around with us as human beings, it is extremely important to shape how people experience tasting itself. That is, if you want to increase the chances of them having a positive experience. Hence the importance I placed on not letting any negative rumors gain any traction. This is important in any business, not just coffee. At the core of it, though, you have to be honest and confident that you are seeking the best possible quality. There is a part of this, when you are seeking the best, that comes back to protect you like rear guard armor. People will be more positive towards you and your product and they will be less critical and fault-finding than they might otherwise be.

Lesson 13

EXCELLENCE WILL PROTECT YOU

Managing the transition to the new coffee with all those store-owners was a good challenge. The next challenge proved to be even more difficult. I was continually racking my brains, trying to figure out how to motivate these people to do a really good job. I had implemented a barista-training program, but much less time was allocated to it than was ideal because the store-owners had to actually be trained how to run their own small business, which included food, money management, staff hiring and rostering, and the other multitude of activities that every small business owner must navigate.

Usually these retail operators had never run their own small business prior to this one. It took me a quite a while to realize that most of them were not like the usual independent, self-starting small business entrepreneurs I was used to dealing with as a wholesaler. They were people who had an idea and the vision to open their own café or restaurant, and who then went out on their own and took the risk of financing it, and sorting through all the red tape and the potential rip-off merchants. They had to have a pretty high appetite for risk. They had to be good at overcoming everyday difficulties and become their own creative problem-solvers.

The very reason most people buy a franchise is because of exactly the opposite reason! They do not have as high an in-built appetite for calculated risk-taking as independent operators. In fact this is often why they buy a franchise in the first place and don't start a business on their own. They at least know themselves sufficiently well enough to avoid getting in too deep without obtaining professional help beforehand. Most of the store-owners came with the mind-set that was a bit like that of a tenant as opposed to a home-owner; they often looked to me, as their supplier, to fix their problems, rather than taking the initiative to fix a problem themselves. Of course, not all of them were like this and the more self-starting the store-owner they were, the better they did.

But I still had to try and figure out how to change a culture and inspire them to create excellent coffee! Explaining the financial benefit of serving a good coffee didn't seem to work in spite of these benefits being pretty impressive. For instance, the average usage per store was only six kilograms per week, and on average, they would get about seventy cups per kilogram. If they sold those cups for say, $4 each, their cost price (i.e. the cost of goods like the coffee, cup, milk, sugar etc.) would be about $1. That would leave about $3 gross profit for them to then pay for wages, rent, insurance, overheads, repairs and maintenance, and hopefully have some savings left over for them as self-employed investors. So seventy cups x $3 works out at about $210 per week. Times that by fifty weeks per year (to allow for holidays) and you have about $10,000 gross profit potential per kilogram per year.

Eventually, we managed to increase the average kilogram usage per store by almost 370 percent, from six kilograms per store per week to about twenty-two kilograms per store. That represented an extra $180,000 gross profit per store across three hundred and fifty stores by the time I finished.

Operating a store as a barista and owner-manager doing six kilograms per week versus one doing over twenty kilograms or forty kilograms or even sixty kilograms per week is completely different. It requires lots of extra skills in order to be able to handle this sort of growth and volume. Overcoming the skill barrier requires lots of training on the job. But it is helpful to think of it in stages.

I encouraged them to think of the building steps for every ten kilograms increase or $100,000 per year extra income they had at their disposal. The first stage is one to ten kilograms per week. This requires only one barista working at a very slow pace most of the time. Eleven to twenty kilograms per week requires a barista who has more speed skills but who won't compromise quality. Twenty-one to forty kilograms is a completely different level and involves breaking down the tasks into their basic elements.

One of the challenges with a café business during the growth phase is that busy patches will vary from day to day until the store is just maxed out all the time. The juggling act is to avoid overstaffing and having staff members under-utilized when there are quiet times. But you also need well-trained staff who can jump on at a moment's notice as soon as a rush of customers comes into the café so they are served quickly and professionally.

You can recognize the professionally trained café staff as they handle the busy rushes calmly and efficiently, often in a conversation-free, but dedicated atmosphere. Good, experienced staff often communicate non-verbally and anticipate customers' and each other's needs. It creates a cool paradox out of a relaxed yet energized vibe that is very attractive and enjoyable. Subconsciously, people, both staff and customers, are reassured and everyone becomes more confident and calm. This is not always so easy to achieve though.

As anyone who loves their coffee served by a barista knows, the coffee can be very variable from one barista to the next. Training is essential to get staff to increase their speed without upsetting customers by either making them wait too long or by cutting corners and not making the coffee well enough. To get multiple baristas to do a coffee menu in as similar a way as possible requires constant training. But it also requires that the owner makes decisions about how they are going to actually train their staff. There are lots of different ways of achieving the same end. But it is necessary to pick one way and stick with it and only modify it when necessary.

Too many changes without clear communication creates confusion and chaos, and is a disaster for any business. A great French war proverb that has sometimes been attributed to Napoleon is "Order, counter-order, disorder," or words to that effect in French anyway. This applies not only to war but also to any business. That is, once you have picked a method of proceeding, don't change it in the middle of operations. Ideally, basic training happens away from the shop floor, when there are no customers around. The next stage is hands-on exposure in the store in quiet times only, and then a steady increase in pressure as the trainee barista is gradually exposed to busier rush times.

Often it is easier to work with someone who has no previous training rather than someone who brings an opinionated attitude and different way of making coffee. There is nothing wrong with experimenting and improving when you have time—in fact it is essential to test alternative methods—but you will always still need to pick one way of making coffee if you want consistency under pressure, even if your baristas are highly skilled and capable of multiple ways of making the same coffee.

As soon as I heard about a government certified course, 'Cert IV: Train The Trainer,' I paid for a professional trainer to come in and train the barista-trainers who were working with me. I had recently hired a new trainer, Rick Carlino, who had previously worked for a burgeoning competitor coffee chain from America. He was a very likeable guy who was proud of his coffee skills to the point that he kept on mentioning how the other company made their coffee just a few too many times. I knew how they made their coffee but I believed we were further down the trail than they were.

One little tiny example that could have become a major problem was that Rick, as a new trainer, used a metal spatula to manipulate how much froth and steamed milk he poured into a given cup. More froth for a cappuccino, less for a caffè latte, and less again for a flat white. This was a technique that had been imported from America. Keep in mind, this was around 2001 or so, and barista skills were pretty basic on a general scale. We were trying to train our baristas to do latte art by free-pouring, which is far more difficult to train and at first appears slower until baristas can develop speed skills. Using a spatula was just not going to cut it. In fact, you don't see baristas using this spatula or spoon technique to hold back froth any more, but it was the industry standard back then. We were trying to change it and go a step ahead.

Just prior to our group 'train-the-trainer' session, I finally snapped when I was with Rick on the training machine and I saw him using a spoon to restrain the milk froth from pouring into a cup yet again. I grabbed the spoon. With a bit of forcefulness, borne out of frustration and annoyance at this backward approach, I told him angrily, "If I ever catch you using a spoon to make a milky coffee again, I will throw it at you!" I might have intended to throw it at the time so he knew I was serious, but I wouldn't have actually hit him—in spite of what I said. But nevertheless, he could tell I passionately meant it when I said it.

Just a couple of hours later, with a very polite trainer who was training me and our trainers on how to communicate effectively and respectfully at all times, Rick and I burst out laughing as we both recalled my rant about his use of the spoon. Clearly it was not how the textbook said you should train someone. Nevertheless, Rick never used a spoon or spatula again and became an excellent trainer. Sometimes a bit of passion works wonders, even if it is not quite by the book. At the very least, this train-the-trainer program lifted the skills of our barista trainers and helped them become more professional and more consistent trainers.

Lesson 14

PASSIONATE EDUCATION WORKS

When interviewing prospective employees who claimed to have skills, I made them do a practical test. As I was trying to figure out how we could best inspire baristas to do a better job, we needed to employ more barista trainers. At that stage of the industry's development, it was really a new career path. I advertised for a new barista trainer, and I narrowed it down in my fast-track way and arranged appointments with the three best applicants.

When they came into the training room, I chatted with them in a relaxed, conversational way to try and get an understanding of what made them tick: what their interests outside of work were; what their ambitions were; where they saw themselves in a few years or five or ten years' time. I then explained to them that obviously, because they were going to have to train others in how to make coffee, they would need to be competent baristas themselves, and asked if they would mind doing a little practical demonstration that consisted of making four coffees in a limited time with only a few minutes to set up. They of course agreed because they wanted the job.

I was amazed at how this simple demonstration separated the wheat from the chaff. There was one particular guy who amazed me as he just kept going for almost ten minutes and still couldn't make one satisfactory coffee. What stunned me wasn't that he was not able to demonstrate the necessary skills, so much as his ability to have no embarrassment about his inappropriate lack of skill. He pretended right up until he walked out the door that he was actually perfectly skilled for the position. It was a great insight into the human ability for creating not just words that do not match up to actions, but actions that don't match up to stated ability. Integrity is important.

In terms of hiring a new barista trainer, I had drawn a blank. None of the people I interviewed where good enough.

At about this time though, I heard about a barista competition that was being staged by a coffee brand in Australia known as Piazza D'Oro, that was owned by Douwe Egberts, a very large European firm. They were real trailblazers of this kind of public barista competition in Australia, and it was certainly the first time I had ever heard of such an event. I was immediately curious to understand what it entailed and as it was open to everyone, I tried to encourage a couple of our baristas to enter, even though one of the stipulations was that the contestants had to use Piazza D'Oro coffee. The competition was interesting and seemed to be based as much around general coffee knowledge as practical barista skills, with the judges interviewing the contestants as well as analyzing their coffee-making ability.

There, I met a young affable guy who had just started his new coffee business by the name of Toby Smith, who of course grew his business, Toby's Estate, into what is now a global brand. I also went and saw Toby's first roasting equipment that was in his mother's Darlinghurst garage: a little five kilogram Turkish model very similar to the roaster my brother had started out with some twenty years before.

I met another young guy there, George Sabados, who was rather charismatic and who was emceeing the competition. I managed subsequently to persuade George to start working with me as my first barista trainer. To this day, I believe George is still one of the best trainers I have ever came across anywhere in the world.

I was intrigued by the way the competition worked and how it seemed to inspire people to do a good job. I knew this was something I desperately needed to do across every one of the seventy stores I was charged with helping to grow. One of the flaws in this format seemed to be that it was run and branded by a company, and didn't allow for different coffees that reflected the barista's own preference. It would have been a bit like the Formula 1 but all the drivers having to compete using only one brand of car. As a branding exercise, it was no doubt very good and visionary for the time, but as a format, it was always going to be limited.

Coincidentally I had also attended another annual Specialty Coffee Association of America conference, which was still the only other place I knew of anywhere in the world where my thirst for new coffee knowledge could be satisfied. I saw a barista competition there that was sponsored by Da Vinci syrups and run by Sherri and Danny Johns. This had a different format again but didn't seem to be quite as coffee focused as the Australian format that I had seen.

After I returned home, I was pondering the different competition formats and the need to combine the coffee dedication of the Australian competition format, and the theatre and entertainment of the signature drink component of the American format. I happened to look through one of only two international coffee trade journals at the time, both of which I used to devour every month. One was called the *Tea and Coffee Trade Journal,* published since 1901, and the other was called *Coffee and Cocoa International* magazine. Those were the only educational coffee publications that I knew of up until then where you could learn more about coffee.

In the *Coffee and Cocoa International* magazine, I saw an advertisement for the inaugural World Barista Championship to be held in Monte Carlo later the same year. I enquired immediately and found out that the format seemed to combine the two elements I had long been thinking about. As it happened, no one else from Australia had enquired about this world championship competition and so, as I was the only person who had taken the time to enquire, I was told I was free to enter a barista on behalf of Australia if I could get there in time.

I consulted with my wife, and she very big-heartedly agreed that we could pay for the trip out of our own personal savings. And so I booked and paid for tickets for George Sabados and me to fly to Monte Carlo.

The format for the competition was pretty simple: make four espresso coffees, four cappuccinos, and four signature coffee drinks that could include any non-alcoholic additional flavorings. The whole performance was to be within a fifteen-minute timeframe.

With minimal practice and some preparation in the form of me purchasing and testing some backup ultra-heat-treated milk, we prepared to set off from Sydney airport with a dozen liter-packs of milk in my suitcase. Before our flight departure, we went to get a coffee from the café that had the best reputation for coffee in the airport. All the flight crews and well-seasoned travelers would go to this one particular café that happened to be the first café in Sydney that was serving a particular Melbourne coffee. That coffee was called Grinders and at the time, the brand was owned and run by the Italian-born founder Giancarlo. He had started his business about five decades previously, roasting and serving coffee in Lygon Street, Melbourne, and was in the vanguard of those great Italian post-World War II immigrant coffee entrepreneurs, who helped transform Australian culture from beer-swilling to latte-sipping.

This one outlet in Sydney International Airport was an amazingly good example of how to break into a new market. After almost five decades toiling nearly six hundred miles away in Melbourne, and remaining pretty much unknown in Sydney, it was amazing how quickly his brand spread into this new market. By being located in the airport through which lots of influential people constantly traveled, and by doing a good job, the word of mouth and demand for his coffee grew rapidly. It was guerrilla marketing by default, sneaking in under the guard of two of the biggest nationally dominant players in their own home city. George and I enjoyed a really good old-school, smooth, rich classic Italian-style espresso and then boarded our plane.

We flew to Monte Carlo with a brief layover in Paris. I left Australia with the starry-eyed view that I was heading to France, the epicenter of world culinary expertise. I expected that this would extend to an experience of fantastic coffees as a result. I was sadly disappointed. Although now almost twenty years later, the French are making large strides to improve the quality of their coffee, at this point in time, when I sought out a good café in Charles De Gaulle airport, for instance, I came away with a very sad and unappealing coffee experience. Sadly it was not much better at any of the French cafés we tried along the way either.

By the time of my return, with the possible exception of the espresso coffees that George and his other seven competitor baristas had made while we were away, it turned out that the humble coffee I was served by the barista at

Sydney airport was one of the best coffees I enjoyed on the whole trip. This was a rather startling revelation to me as to how much the appreciation for good coffee had grown in Australia. It was not clear then to what extent this would continue, but this growth has not slowed in the intervening decades. It has actually increased exponentially on the back of tens of thousands of small coffee entrepreneurs who have all passionately and with varying degrees of success, set out to satisfy their curiosity and the ever more sophisticated demand by Australian consumers for great coffee.

Even though it seemed apparent to me that George was probably the most advanced barista at this inaugural World Barista Championship, he ended up fourth after his uncharacteristically nervous performance. The fallback plan of having tested and brought over backup UHT milk was actually a good idea. As it turned out, the finals were held on a Sunday and most of the shops in Monte Carlo were closed on this Sabbath day, so it was almost impossible to get any of the fresh milk that we were used to using.

Unfortunately, about nine of the ten-liter packs of UHT milk had burst on the flight over. So not only did we have just one backup liter of milk, my suitcase had spent much of our stay in our hotel room constantly being washed in the shower! It was the only way I could think of to try and get rid of the sour, curdling nine liters of milk that had leaked all through my suitcase.

On the flight home, in spite of being bitterly disappointed at our misfortune over not winning, my competitive instinct had been aroused, and I resolved to somehow win this world competition. The exposure to this larger world coffee stage inspired me enormously, and supercharged my thirst to learn.

Lesson 15

STAY OPEN
TO LEARNING
NEW THINGS

One of the beauties of coffee is that there is always more to learn about it because it is such an incredibly complex and wonderful natural substance. But in addition, the coffee industry has so many layers to it that there is always more to learn from a business perspective as well.

The coffee grower has to know about agronomy, horticulture, and the processing of the cherry and the bean on the farm in order to make sure that the potential flavor is enhanced. Then the dry-mill operators and exporters add further business fields of expertise in logistics, handling, and marketing. The importer and roaster have to do their magic in the country where the coffee is drunk to again hopefully tease out the hidden intrinsic flavor potential of each bean. A further layer of complexity with coffee that doesn't occur at all in wine, the nearest liquid cousin to coffee, is the huge range of brewing equipment that exists to extract the liquid coffee through the dry-roasted beans. As a result, the specialty coffee industry seems to attract an extremely eclectic range of people, from ex-lawyers, to accountants, to financial industry whizz kids, nerds, and engineers, to dreamers, artists, and even history students. The history of coffee and its current economic importance is truly astounding. There is a strikingly common theme though among all coffee entrepreneurs who thrive regardless of their background, and that is the hunger to learn more about not just coffee, but also about how to run a successful business.

While in Monte Carlo, I was asked to join the new steering committee for the World Barista Championship (WBC), which included some Americans and some Europeans. This gave me an opportunity to have input into the development of what has now become the formal rules and regulations for the World Barista Championship. It also enabled me to keep in contact with a newly emerging international specialty coffee community and the progression of barista techniques.

Seeing the birth of a new venture in the form of an ambitious world barista competition, initiated mainly by Scandinavian coffee entrepreneurs, and seeing how it grew to become a substantial, globally influential business force, has been very interesting to say the least. Baristas who win can make a lot of money for themselves and the companies who have helped them get there. All this growth has also coincided with the meteoric rise of smartphone technology and the explosion of social media. This has all catalyzed to form a very exciting era for coffee entrepreneurs globally.

After arriving back in Sydney, some of the barista evaluation tools I had been using for our baristas were absorbed into the WBC rules and conversely, I set about spreading this passion for coffee into our store-owner system using the competition format. I had racked my brains, trying to figure out how to inspire store-owners who had often mortgaged their homes or invested their life savings to give themselves a start as coffee entrepreneurs and small business proprietors. I knew if they could become passionate about executing good coffee then they would most likely be better off financially.

We used to train store-owners to make a good coffee, and as I've said, to refrain from serving a sub-standard one and then having to redo their coffee if necessary. When this dedication is coupled with good hospitality skills, it is a winning combination. It is the secret behind why two apparently identical stores in the same area can be completely different. One will be really busy and packed with customers and the other store that doesn't get this, will emanate a forlorn lonely aura.

In spite of this, it was still proving very hard to get store-owners to understand that all this extra attention taken to make a good coffee was worthwhile. I decided to hold our own internal barista championship along the lines of the World Barista Championship format. We made it compulsory for every store to enter a barista in the competition. We tried to make sure that the owner of the store or one of their working relatives was the competitor. We knew if they improved, they would be more likely to become the enforcer of coffee standards in their own store and could make sure all their casual staff conformed to the desired standards long after we had finished our training session and when we couldn't be physically present. This is a really important business principle.

Lesson 16

TRAIN THE BOSS AND LET THEM ENFORCE QUALITY

In the meantime, we set about organizing the competition demonstrations in key stores in the evenings after business hours. We insisted that only the owners attend and that no more than three or four nearby store-owners attend as well. We would then walk into the store, explain the competition rules, and demonstrate in front of them how to make four espressos, four cappuccinos, and four 'signature drinks' in twelve minutes. This was the world championship format except that we shortened the timeframe from fifteen minutes to twelve because we wanted to make it more commercially relevant. We figured that if a barista couldn't serve twelve coffees in at least twelve minutes, they would not be of use in a busy store and should get another job.

A remarkable thing happened as a result. Some of the most truculent and difficult store-owners were humbled in front of their peers. Often the difficult people who complained the loudest had the poorest skills. It was like in the movie *The Wizard of Oz* where the curtain is drawn open and the big, intimidating bully is revealed to be a small inconsequential ordinary person. Newer more impressionable store-owners suddenly realized their noisy, domineering, seemingly know-it-all peers were not so intimidating. The store-owners who were willing to learn new techniques and who were open to improving themselves eventually found their businesses did really well, particularly the ones who had done well in the competitions. This was partly because the same skills that enabled someone to win a barista competition, also enabled them to improve their coffee quality and the tangible culture of their staff. Eventually, good culture prevailed and dominated.

As the troublesome store-owners who didn't embrace the new competitive culture found, their businesses stagnated. They simultaneously saw their peers, many of them much less experienced, grow their customer base, improve the staff morale, and have more valuable businesses. The stick-in-the-mud old operators would then often humble themselves in private, and seek out their new peers and ask them what the key to their success was. They found out that it was actually pretty simple. Be pleasant to customers, keep the store clean, and improve your skills to make sure the quality of the coffee is as good as possible. It's called *hospitality!*

The competitions created local heroes because we made sure they got public relations coverage in their local newspapers. Again, this was before social media, but the effect was electrifying at the time. The local barista hero had new customers coming to his store to sample their coffee, and when they found that the store actually did deliver a really good coffee, they kept coming back for more and the businesses boomed. The other store-owners saw their success and wanted to emulate it. The dynamic within the whole chain became positive, where everyone was competing to out-succeed their peers in a healthy way: by making a better coffee! These days social media only serves to amplify and accelerate this whole dynamic.

Obviously there was a lot more to it behind the scenes, but in the space of a few short years, the entire business culture was changed completely. It fitted in with my personal goal of trying to democratize the experience of good coffee for all Australians, rather than it being a rare and haphazard occurrence as it was by and large in Australia in the late 1990s. I envisioned that even ordinary mainstream cafés in shopping centers would have excellent coffees on offer. Even though there is still a long way to go, the quality and dedication of baristas has certainly improved in this time, as has the international reputation of Australian coffee.

I grew enormously as well. I invested time and money in traveling to the other side of the world several times a year to keep in touch with both the Specialty Coffee Associations in America and Europe as I kept working on the committee for the World Barista Championship. I also started going to the newly formed Cup of Excellence coffee competitions. These competitions were organized to help showcase unique specialty coffees from growing countries, starting in Brazil and then spreading to Central America and beyond.

I was committed to pushing myself to the limit in regard to learning about coffee and doing the best I possibly could with my coffee business. I also came back from Monte Carlo with my competitive instinct fired up in the knowledge that Australia was actually ahead of the curve in many ways with our espresso-based coffee culture, and winning the World Barista Championship could be a way of proving it.

I dedicated myself to winning this competition. Soon afterwards, I was elected chairman of the Australian Coffee and Tea Association, and I set about running Australia's first national barista championship. This was a very humble affair held near Fox Studios in Sydney with the help of Toby Smith, George Sabados, and Emily Oak, among others. The winner that year was a barista by the name of Corinne Tweedale, who was working as a barista trainer for a competitor coffee chain at the time but who prior to this had managed my old Neutral Bay café.

The astounding result of this competition was that for the first time, it attracted mainstream news media and a photo of her win featured prominently in one of the main Sydney newspapers. Some serious people took notice of this little competition.

Even though many of the members of this old-school association hadn't been able to understand the need for barista competitions, one member in particular, as a result of the surprising level of media interest, wanted to own and control it for himself. He used a flimsy pretext of 'conflict of interest' in relation to my position as Chairman, even though it was an unpaid one, and tried to sue me.

As a result, I resigned as chairman of the old-school coffee association, and with George Sabados, set up a new not-for-profit one, that is now known as the Australian Specialty Coffee Association, specifically to keep running the coffee competitions. But even though this aggressive guy dropped the lawsuit against me, he flew to Oslo, Norway and tried to convince the WBC organizers to give him the sole Australian rights to the competition for his company. Thankfully they said they were happy with the not-for-profit work George and I were doing and a big Norwegian Viking stood up to this Australian bully.

The following year, 2002, the WBC was to be held in Oslo. I knew if I was to stay in touch with the latest world developments, I had to be there. I was still on the world organizing committee. The trouble was, a colleague in the business was upset that I was traveling overseas so much now and he wasn't. My business partners who also owned the patisserie chain had limited my overseas trips to one per year in the company budget. Unfortunately, I had already traveled to America for the SCAA coffee conference, so how was I to get to Oslo to keep in the race for the world barista competition? I decided to use my frequent flyer points to pay for the trip. But I wasn't sure how to get time away from the coffee factory to go there?

I decided to fly to Norway for the weekend. That doesn't sound like such a big deal if you live in the northern hemisphere, but when you live Down Under it means a very long-haul flight. And I mean long! Flying anywhere in the world from Australia means a long-haul flight, with the exception of flying to New Zealand. A flight from Sydney to Oslo takes more than thirty-two hours one-way!

I packed my bags and flew out on a Thursday evening and arrived in Oslo on Saturday morning. I went straight to the competition area from the airport and joined in with the judging. I worked, and caught up with my friends and colleagues from around the world who were involved in the competition that year at a party later that night on an island near Oslo.

I also came across Paul Bassett, who was the Australian competitor that year. He came up to me and asked my opinion on a coffee that he got me to taste. I commented that it seemed a little under-roasted and thought nothing more of it. It turned out that it was his coffee that he was using in the competition and unbeknown to me, he had some doubts about it. Paul missed out on the finals that year.

I helped judge the finals and as the awards were being announced, left the competition stage and headed straight back to the airport for my thirty-two hour journey o Australia. I arrived at six a.m. on Tuesday morning, and went straight from the airport to my coffee factory in western Sydney and worked a full day. As far as my work colleagues were concerned, I had been away for a long weekend. What a long weekend!

It's funny how when you push yourself to the limit, good things come back to you. As a result of going to Oslo, Paul Basset subsequently approached me to help with his coffee and a tilt at the next year's world barista championship. I gladly worked with Paul and put together a blend that included the winning Cup of Excellence Guatemala coffee for that year. I'm pretty sure this was the first time such a special coffee was used in a barista competition anywhere in the world. Paul was incredibly dedicated and devoted a large part of his time that year to succeeding. I supported him and his wife to go to Boston for the 2003 World Barista Championship, which he duly won. This resulted in a mutually fruitful relationship that has lasted for a long time.

Back in the early 2000s, there were not many qualified barista trainers though, and their skill set tended to be limited to classroom situations. We sent our barista trainers out on the road. Initially, every three months they had to visit every store in their area and fill out a written checklist of all the relevant skills and items the store-owner should have in place. It wasn't a secret shopper program, but because often the store was busy, the store operators wouldn't at first notice the trainer near their store and they could observe a lot while watching a barista in operation when they were not aware of a spectator.

In this way, almost half the evaluation could often be completed by the time the trainer stepped inside the store. Many of the details of these evaluations became a part and parcel of the World Barista Championship rules that I was collaborating on with my international friends, like tamping techniques, and cleanliness and grinder management.

Once inside the store, it became a rather sensitive issue when you had to explain to a store-owner where their shortcomings might be. If this was not done in person at the time, it could blow up into a major conflict later on. Ultimately, when this hard news was sympathetically communicated, the store-owners responded positively to remedial training. We made free re-training available in the evening after closing time at our training facility on a regular basis so any staff could do a refresher course or explore more advanced skills. It worked. A few years later, we were independently rated as the number-one coffee chain in the nation by BIS Shrapnel, better than the coffee specialist chains.

This systematic approach to establishing a preventative service checklist and quality maintenance program was coupled with an overall five-star rating program for every store, initiated by Chris Fitzmaurice. It was a very powerful and effective tool in helping motivate store-owners. It meant that if they gained a good rating, it made their stores more attractive and valuable to prospective buyers.

In 2002, I met Dr Ernesto Illy at an SCAA conference after he spoke as a coffee luminary. Someone asked him his opinion on which was the best espresso machine. I leaned in to hear his softly spoken response. In a very gentlemanly manner, with a refined Italian accent, he explained, "The best espresso machine is the one with the best backup." I was struck by this simple yet wise reply.

Following on from Dr Illy's advice about the best coffee machine being the one with the best backup, I chose machines from a guy called Mike Delzoppo. Not because his were necessarily the best, but because he was honest and supported his machines well, and was willing to be innovative. Mike had started as a humble coffee machine technician in Melbourne as a young man and had developed his business to the point where he was importing machines and providing machine service and maintenance nationally.

Together we came up with a preventative maintenance program. My business partners and I made sure that every store received up to four free machine services a year based on how much coffee they went through. As a result, Mike's technicians could plan their weekly runs and be way more productive. Rather than running from one side of a large city to the other for two emergency breakdown callouts in a day, they could now do five or six preventative maintenance calls a day, which resulted in far less breakdowns. This resulted in a reduction in time-wasting emergency callouts for the technicians. Mike saved a lot of money, his technicians were way more productive, and our machines broke down less often than our competitors'. We dubbed it the 'safety-net servicing program' and giving some of it away for free worked!

It sounds simple, but our competitors weren't doing this because they were looking at their businesses differently. They didn't want to pay for the servicing of their store-owners' coffee equipment. We made sure we had strict controls in place so the program didn't get abused. We only covered the callout fee and one hour's labor fee, which is all the time it should normally take for a service if it is done regularly. And we only paid for the work done within normal business hours. If the store-owner wanted it done after hours, they had to pay the difference. They also had to pay for spare parts, so this kept a lid on unnecessary replacements. The program worked. I likened our competitors to someone looking down a telescope from the wrong end. They saw the cost of machine servicing as just that: a cost. I viewed it as an investment. It was an investment in building better businesses for everyone concerned. It was a genuine win-win result and a part of the basis for it was actually simple generosity. By giving something away for free, we actually received much more back.

Picture what happens when a coffee machine breaks down: the customer is still going to want their morning coffee, so they will have their coffee somewhere else that they haven't tried before. Over time, mixed with the good PR we were getting from the coffee competitions, people would try us when a competitor's machine failed. If our store was up to speed with their skills, thanks to the free training available to them, the store would invariably keep these new customers as ongoing patrons. In fact, in the five-year period that our per-store sales increased by 370 percent, I know of one major competitor whose sales declined by 40 percent at exactly the same time. Go figure!

Another benefit of the free machine-service program was that it acted like a de-facto coffee audit. We set it up so that the store-owner had to sign the checklist once the work was done to keep the technicians honest and to verify that it was okay for us to pay their bill. We also received a copy so we could see how the store's equipment was holding up. It helped us to flush out poor operators.

One example was when I got a call from Barry at Bankstown complaining that his coffee was tasting bad. I had once previously caught out Barry substituting a cheaper competitor roast of coffee in his store when I had visited him, and I noticed that there was a residue of different color roast grinds lying around the grinder. He hadn't even bothered to try and cover his tracks before I arrived at his store. Having called his bluff on cheating the system once before, I was pretty confident there wasn't a problem with the coffee, particularly as the other three hundred or so stores weren't having any issues.

I went dutifully out to the store and while Barry was distracted by his customers, I noticed there was a service sticker on the grinder saying he had refused the technician's service for his grinder. I found out that Barry didn't want to pay the $250 for new grinder blades and was operating with worn-out blades, which any self-respecting barista will tell you makes for lousy-tasting coffee. These days, this could be monitored by using a refractometer, but in any case, thanks to the technician's preventative maintenance call, we told Barry to stop wasting everyone's time and ruining his own business and invest in new grinder blades.

Barry very penitently agreed to sort his blades out. The follow-up to this story is that some people just don't get it! As it turned out, Barry went and bought some cheaper $100 unbranded, non-genuine blades that of course caused him even more grief when they didn't work properly. I told Barry to pay the extra and invest in genuine blades and get on with building his business. Sometimes there is no way of changing or helping a character when they are their own worst enemy.

So, if there are two ways of viewing the cost of servicing coffee machines, then there are also two ways of viewing a business. As I said, one of our main competitor's businesses declined by 40 percent per store across three hundred stores in the same period when our business increased by 370 percent across three hundred and fifty stores. Clearly the people in charge of our business viewed some costs differently. Even though it is in fact more likely that a fish rots from its gut first and not its head, in business, there is a case to argue that those in charge of the business create the culture.

By viewing the machine-servicing costs as an investment in a range of benefits, as opposed to just viewing them as a mere cost to the business, it enabled us to be much more profitable. We sold more coffee and the store-owners had more savings/profit at their disposal. Everyone in our system won, whereas our competitors declined.

Lesson 17

SOW GENEROUSLY AND YOU WILL REAP GENEROUSLY

Winston Churchill is quoted as having once said, "Success consists of going from failure to failure without loss of enthusiasm." Certainly, it is hard to maintain enthusiasm when things don't go your way. But it is important to learn the lessons so hopefully we can avoid going from failure to failure, and eventually go onto success!

At the height of my success, I was a part-owner in a coffee-roasting business that supplied about three hundred and fifty in-house stores. The business was making a lot more than it was spending, and pretty much everyone associated with the coffee that we produced was likewise doing a good job and making a lot more than they were spending.

Then one of my business partners had a serious heart attack and was clinically dead for several minutes. Thankfully, he was revived and did not suffer any brain damage, but he did have to have a pacemaker permanently inserted in his chest. Not long after this, he suggested I might want to think about the possibility of selling out of the business. I wasn't too interested in the idea at all.

It turned out, even though I wasn't aware at the time, my partners wanted to join our completely independent coffee business together with their main franchise business, as that would make it easier and more valuable to sell the business as a package deal to investors. In the process, I was laid off without pay a few weeks before Christmas and then we were at a stand-off—and so the negotiations began. They soon made me an offer for my shares in the company but I thought their value was worth a lot more and so I declined their offer. One issue then was that, according to my lawyer's advice, I should stay on as a director to enable me to remain informed about the business. This meant I was limited to the kind of work I could earn money from because of potential conflicts of interest. And in fact I did get a job offer from the other main international coffee competitor in Australia within a couple of weeks. I declined the offer in spite of the allure of the replacement income.

An even larger problem in my mind was that I had four children who were in good private schools with expensive school fees, a new house with a large mortgage, an investment property, and not enough income to cover the costs of this lifestyle. In retrospect, I should have sold the larger second house straight away and reduced our loan expenses. I could then have probably hung on without taking the kids out of the very good schools they were attending and have avoided disrupting their lives too much. It would have been humbling, but it took quite a while to realize this was even necessary. In the meantime, the debts were mounting up and the negotiations stalled. Having less income than expenses is a very stressful way of living.

At the same time though, I figured I could open a new café near to where we lived and not have any conflict with my directorship of the wholesale coffee-roasting business. I approached my brother-in-law, Rob, who was interested in investing in a coffee business with me. Rob was a successful and hardworking executive in the financial services industry. Little did I know that later on he would subsequently become a thorough coffee professional in his own right! At this point in my career though, I had established two successful wholesale coffee-roasting businesses and three of my own successful cafés in the competitive Sydney market, and helped establish training and support systems for hundreds of coffee entrepreneurs with their own successful cafés nationally. All this in just over twenty years, and I felt very confident I could open one single new café successfully. How wrong I was!

I made so many rookie errors it was embarrassing. I tried to merge together a new concept store that could potentially be replicated and possibly franchised. The idea was to offer a range of alternative healthy fresh salads, a range of different-flavored Australian-style meat pies, and of course, great coffee. The idea was bad! The type of customers who eat healthy salads and the type of customers who eat Australian meat pies are two completely different tribes. It is true they both love good coffee, but together, it made for a conflicted retail offering and the store lost money from the start.

When your personal expenses are more than your earnings, you make a loss. When your business expenses are more than your earnings, you also make a loss. Combine the two and your losses really mount up quickly, and they hurt. This was where I found myself in a very short amount of time. This is also why businesses must have a profit and loss report or P&L. I had always made sure I had a good bookkeeper who gave me an accurate monthly P&L, but unfortunately, no matter how hard I tried to improve the business, it kept on floundering on the big 'loss' side!

Losing money is very demoralizing. It makes the allure of a realistic profit very appealing, whether the word *profit* has a dirty connotation or not. In addition, having personal losses is even more painful than having business ones. The idea of actually making a personal profit becomes a very real and urgent necessity. Ask any family who can't pay their bills. It is bloody painful, if you have a conscience.

As the losses mounted, I tried anything I could to make ends meet, including international consulting, but I couldn't cut the deadweight of a shop that was dragging me further and further underwater financially. I tried selling it to different people but of course, as anybody who has tried knows, it is very hard to sell a business that is losing money. I had signed up for a six-year property lease in a small shopping center where the rent was too high. It was like a prison sentence where I was being tortured daily.

I had to make really unpleasant phone calls to the Australian Tax Office because I couldn't pay them the money I owed. I needed it to put food on the table. That was really hard. But to their credit, the tax office personnel who I spoke to were invariably personable and sympathetic which, still to this day, I am grateful for. At a time when I felt so vulnerable and stressed, it made a difference to have someone sympathetic on the other end of the line.

Eventually after almost twenty months of negotiations, my business partners offered me the same amount as they had in the first couple of weeks of our negotiations. By this time, I think they sensed I was worn out and at the end of my rope financially, and I caved in and accepted their offer. What I didn't know was that if I had been able to hang on for another six months or so, I may have got the figure I had in mind and which I thought was fair. This would have enabled me to pay off all my debt and have some funds left over to invest. Because my partners wanted to bundle the two businesses together in order to sell them as one package, I would have been the sticking point holding up their deal. As it happened, they ended up receiving about $48 million for the combined businesses of which the coffee business was probably worth about $16 million. I received only a tiny fraction of this, which was not even enough to clear out my debts. I had managed to hang on to our family home and had sold the small investment property, but my personal monthly P&L and my new shop's P&L were both still decidedly in the ongoing red. In other words, I was still making losses every month on both fronts.

In the meantime, I didn't let the grass grow under my feet as I still managed to travel to the specialty coffee conferences in America each year and kept working on the World Barista Championship committee. I had also been the first Australian to judge coffees at the Cup of Excellence competitions for growers in Guatemala, El Salvador, and Nicaragua.

I navigated the international coffee politics necessary to have a tilt for the role as the executive director of the World Barista Championship. My final job interview for this role was rather unusual.

I applied for the role in 2004 just after my impasse began with my business partners. As it happened, the interview process was conducted in Illy Caffè's headquarters in Trieste, Italy. Prior to walking into the boardroom, I waited in the staff cafeteria which was the most stylish staff facility I have seen anywhere in the world. Black-tie baristas were available throughout the day to personally serve staff whenever they needed a coffee. The espresso bar itself appeared to be one continuous piece of hand-beaten metal that curved lengthwise and down to the floor. It would probably have been one of the most stylish and impressive bars anywhere, let alone inside a corporate office. It must've made the staff feel special and proud of who they worked for.

Lesson 18

TRY AND MAKE YOUR COLLEAGUES PROUD TO WORK WITH YOU

Applying for the role of executive director of the WBC was the only job interview I ever went for in my coffee career. My previous ones had only been as a teenager applying for unskilled jobs. In this case, I had a thorough knowledge of the role I was applying for, having attended every previous WBC competition, including the inaugural event in Monte Carlo in 2000 when I had been invited to join the steering committee to develop the rules and format.

After contributing to this committee and judging competitors at the subsequent competitions in Miami, Oslo, and Boston, where my barista Paul Bassett won the title and became Australia's first world barista champion, it had become obvious that the championship had grown to the point where it required more formal leadership. And so the position of Executive Director was advertised. Finding myself with spare time on my hands due to the hiatus with my own business, I decided to apply for the role.

It was almost like applying for a political role because the WBC was jointly owned by the American and European specialty coffee associations. The associations were not-for-profit industry organizations run by a handful of paid staff and lots of volunteers. Needless to say, there were a lot of people vying for control of the one global entity they mutually owned. I attended both associations' national conventions and met with all the main players involved in the game at the time. I understood the Scandinavians, who were the prime movers in the beginning of the WBC, were key.

My key Scandinavian ally was Jens Norgaard, from Cafe Europa in Copenhagen, who is a very intelligent and accomplished businessman and coffee entrepreneur with a great sense of fun and a very astute understanding of human nature. With Jens on my side, I navigated the tensions between Europe and America. He introduced me to a key outsider on the selection panel who was also the CEO of Illy Caffè at the time. I met this man at a coffee conference in Atlanta, Georgia, well before the selection interview in Trieste. He seemed like an amiable enough Italian gentleman, but as I put my hand out to shake his, I sensed an emotional change take place. It was like a virtual suit of protective emotional armor snapping shut over his entire body. This guy was a serious, battle-hardened international corporate warrior. He was the executive largely responsible for delivering Ernesto Illy's expansive global vision for Illy Caffè and making it a hard, practical reality.

Dr Ernesto Illy is an example of a great coffee entrepreneur. He studied chemistry at the University of Bologna and had a rare mix of gifts that combined his technical expertise with an astute sense of stylish marketing. He launched innovations like pressurized can packaging to solve the problem of keeping his coffee from staling as it was being transported to his expanding customer base.

He also instituted coffee competitions for growers to reward them for producing better quality. This in turn was an inspiration for later coffee programs like Cup of Excellence that still run to this day, and which directly reward growers for higher quality coffee. I recall being in El Salvador for their inaugural Cup of Excellence competition and a grower who was trying to convince me to buy his coffee proudly displayed his Illy certificate as his credential to prove his dedication to quality.

Dr Illy's legacy was passed onto his son Andreas, who was responsible for the Illy coffee cup art collection, engaging artists to put their creativity to work decorating ordinary coffee cups and transforming them into works of art. This is great marketing as well as being very stylish.

The day before the interview in Trieste, Italy, I discovered that the previous ad hoc executive director of the WBC was going to be on the selection panel. He was a very dominating and powerfully charismatic character. This disturbed me, as I was conscious that even though he had been successful in growing the organization from birth to its current size, he was, in my view, a part of the restraint that was also holding the organization back from becoming more expansive.

As I sat waiting to be called into the boardroom for my interview, admiring the beautiful in-house espresso bar at Illy's headquarters, this very imposing Viking-like previous executive director walked in. He sat down next to me and in a very seductive tone, attempted to beguile me with his skillful and likeable friendliness. He seemed to be trying to reassure me that I had nothing to worry about in regard to him. The reality was that I had everything to worry about him, as he walked charismatically into the boardroom before me. I resolved to fix the problem at the source.

Finally, I was called into the boardroom. I walked to the head of the gleaming long wooden table with the international panel of interviewers lined along the sides, including the previous executive director and the Illy corporate warrior CEO. Without even sitting down, I made my intent known. I said that I believed it wasn't appropriate for the previous executive director to be a part of the interview process, as it would distort the discussion necessary for the future benefit of the organization.

I then informed the panel, without sitting down, that I would go back outside and wait for five minutes and that if they wanted the interview with me to continue, they should come out and let me know in that time frame or otherwise I would be on the next airplane back to Australia. I then walked straight out of the boardroom.

I had resolved that the position would actually be unfeasible if I had to deal with this other guy influencing every decision and figured that I could simply do something else if they didn't want to interview me.

As it turned out, within a few minutes, the previous executive director exited the boardroom with a rather defeated air and nodded at me ruefully as he walked past.

I was then called into the boardroom, interviewed, and appointed as the new executive director of the World Barista Championship.

I guess one of the main lessons with this is to back yourself if you believe you are right. It would have been easier for me to avoid the confrontation, but it would not have been in the organization's best interests, and I believe it would have made my role untenable if I hadn't made a stand. Sometimes this is not easy but it is worth taking the risk in the long run.

Lesson 19

BACK
YOURSELF

I kept myself busy by also using this time to write a book called the *Espresso Quest*, detailing my exploration of the complexities of producing a good espresso coffee and I helped Vince Piccolo set up his new roasting facility in Vancouver called 49th Parallel coffee roasters.

With all this travel though, it didn't take long to chew into the new capital savings. My old business partners asked me to come back and do my job again but this time as a contractor rather than a business partner. As humbling as this may have seemed, I was grateful for the offer, and after almost two years, jumped back into the saddle in the same factory and business I had previously set up as an owner. I didn't and still don't hold any grudge towards my former business partners. They started their business from nothing themselves, and they played the game very hard and they won. Business can be a brutal game though. I had played the game of my own volition as well, and I guess as a result, if nothing else, I was much more sympathetic to the effects of my actions on my brother's situation as a result.

I threw myself into refreshing the factory systems by outsourcing packing of small hand-packs to my former business partner Scott Jones and his business partner at the time, Saxon Wright, who used to work in my old factory in Brookvale while a student years previously. Saxon has gone on to grow his own business known as Pablo & Rusty's. He is now a seriously successful coffee entrepreneur in his own right. Scott has likewise gone on to succeed as a coffee entrepreneur with his business Black Drum Coffee Roasters. In the meantime, I reorganized the barista trainers who were all based in Sydney and traveling interstate to train store-owners nationally. I put the case to the new owners, who had taken over the business almost immediately once my old partners promptly and happily retired.

As it was, the interstate store-owners were not really getting the support they needed and our travel expenses were very high for training support. I recommended reducing the travel expenses and employing new head barista trainers for each state so they could be on the ground locally to ensure the high quality levels were maintained. It was impossible to do this having them all based in one state only. Our Melbourne barista trainer, Zoe, went on to marry Dave Makin who I first met in Bern, Switzerland, at the 2006 World Barista Championship as the Australian champion. Dave and Zoe have together gone on to become accomplished coffee entrepreneurs with their business Axil Coffee Roasters in Melbourne.

These interstate owners ended up buying the entire business. I've got to say, the new owners were great to work with. The main man, Stuart James, was someone who I got on with particularly well. Stuart was an interesting self-made entrepreneur.

He started out as an electrical apprentice working for

BHP in Wollongong, south of Sydney. BHP is one of the world's largest mining and industrial companies. Stuart played rugby league in his youth and was a solidly built guy, and his father was a university lecturer. He had a very sharp business brain underneath his big cheery, bluff, exterior. After finishing his electrical apprenticeship, he figured that being an electrician wasn't for him and he got a job working as an area retail manager for Mister Minit who run shoe-repair, key-cutting, and engraving stores.

He was so successful as a young executive that he was very quickly promoted through the ranks and soon was running Mister Minit Australia-wide. In fact he was managing the national business so successfully that Mister Minit head office flew executives out from Europe to study the secrets to his success. He ran a very lean no-frills business and would fly economy rather than business class to save expenses. In the end, Stuart resigned because he was looking for further opportunities and he was upset by a lot of things, one of which was management allocating their European expensive business-class flights for their fact finding mission to his Australian business. I'm sure this is probably not how they always run their business, but these particular executives got it wrong in Stuart's case.

After resigning from Mister Minit in his early thirties, with a golden handshake, he and a couple of friends, took over the state of Victoria master franchise for the patisserie chain I was supplying coffee to. But there were horror stories of shop fit-outs not being completed properly, and general dissatisfaction at the lack of support from the previous Victorian owner.

I first met him when he came in for barista training in preparation for taking over his new master franchisor territory, along with his two business partners and friends, Nick and Jon. Little did I know how I would be affected by this relationship. We had a lot of fun together in that session, and I made a point of flying interstate to help support them as much as I could. I watched closely as Stuart and his mates sorted resolutely through their problems, one by one. Sometimes this meant packing bakery orders until one a.m. in the morning. I tried to help them wherever I could, even with packing pastry orders, and I would usually stay with them in their homes. This saved their business precious money in its early stages and also enabled us to get to know each other much better than if I'd stayed in a hotel.

I saw Stuart's generosity in trying to help struggling store-owners. He would make resources available, whether it was free barista training with me, which I was happy to offer, or debt relief for cash-strapped operators. He asked for their patience, commitment, and cooperation in return, and invariably these struggling operators ended up succeeding if they stuck to his program. Anyone who was obstructive or unwilling to cooperate was quickly moved on. The unavoidable legal challenges they inherited were met head-on and dealt with as quickly as possible too. This actually resulted in almost 30 percent of their stores having to close and was very tough because in order to make their business model work, they needed about a minimum of twenty stores for the economies of scale to become viable. Now they were down to about fourteen stores and in a very risky situation. It takes a lot of courage and clear vision to persevere in situations like this. As it happens, these are absolutely indispensable characteristics for any entrepreneur.

Being your own boss is often a two-edged sword. Your problems don't go away at home at night; you tend to mentally chew over the challenges of the day. How am I going to keep this difficult customer happy? What if I lose business to my competitors? At first, it seems stressful. Some people can't get used to this pressure. It is, however, a part of the territory for entrepreneurs. Eventually we mature and become more used to risk. It is a more adventurous way to live. It is important to never become blasé or complacent though, and it is possible to actually become comfortable with the extra risks this working lifestyle entails.

Of course the risk/reward ratio can be much higher. Sometimes business owners who don't take the risk to invest their talents and who remain in that unchallenging, boring job can become envious and jealous of the rewards that many successful entrepreneurs enjoy. As long as the entrepreneur has achieved their goals honestly, they can often find themselves in the position of being able to enjoy the fruits of their labor and even give back far more to their communities, that sustain them.

Eventually, Stuart and his mates' hard work, which also frequently involved getting into stores and serving customers themselves, meant that they opened new stores. And soon they were up to fifty stores and flying along with lots of good success stories under their belts. Then they bought out the Queensland state master franchisor and likewise built that territory up as well, until they had almost one hundred stores under their care.

Two of the first things I did for these new owners were actually diametrically opposed. I decentralized the training by appointing interstate trainers, as I mentioned previously. This improved the level of barista skills nationally with little extra cost, as we saved on flights and accommodation. At the same time, I centralized distribution nationally, by outsourcing it to a specialist distributor who had up until then only been doing our local state distribution. Previously, coffee was sent directly from the factory to each of the individual distributors in each state. By handing this responsibility over to one national distributer and giving them the responsibility of liaising with the interstate distributors, it meant we ended up with better control over our stock and could track and reconcile it much more efficiently. More importantly, we spent less time on unproductive delivery issues and more time focused on producing great coffee.

There were a few other little messy time-wasting details that I adjusted, like free coffee packs being sent to individual stores to reimburse them for ongoing promotional rebates. This meant really fiddly details were being completed by our factory staff, including individual store-owners coming in to the factory to pick up individual one kilogram packs when we were in the middle of trying to roast and pack over seven tons of coffee each week. Eventually I got the accounts department to just credit the stores for the cost of the packs of coffee, which was the same promotional value to the store-owners, and we eliminated a lot of interruptions and wasted time and effort.

All this meant we could concentrate solely on roasting, tasting, and packing the best possible espresso coffee. And this we attempted to do with everything we had. We won a number of awards, and even purchased the winning Cup of Excellence coffee from Brazil for a world-record price at the time. All this resulted in many very successful store-owners and coffee entrepreneurs.

It also gave us time to think about new ways of building the coffee business. For instance, we conducted experiments to evaluate how much decaf coffee we could sell if stores had a good grinder to do it properly instead of treating decaf like a second-class citizen. Stuart immediately authorized the purchase of twenty expensive coffee grinders, and I allocated them to the most deserving stores. We found that after three months, the stores sold significantly more decaf because not only did the decaf taste better, but the decaf drinkers felt respected. The result was an almost 400 percent increase in decaf sales. Many pregnant women, for instance, who love their coffee but are concerned about caffeine loved it and would bring in their social circle of friends with them. I calculated that we would pay off the cost of the grinders in a very short time and Stuart very quickly made certain that every new store that opened had an extra grinder included for free as part of their equipment. This is a really good example of a franchisor doing the right thing by helping out a store-owner at his own expense, but it also happens to be the smart thing from a business point of view because everyone is better off. Whenever you can create a win-win outcome and it is ethical, go for it!

I knew Stuart was ambitious as he had already told me he had been investigating international opportunities in countries like Canada, and he'd also had previous international experience with his role at Mister Minit. He certainly brought his vision and successful energy to the business as a whole by inaugurating the first national conference, and he always appreciated it if I brought something to the table that was 'outside the box.' I enjoyed the challenge of innovating and making the coffee business the best it could be. The future looked exciting as we headed off to Hayman Island Resort in the beautiful Whitsundays for our annual national conference.

Unfortunately, sometimes life hands out some very tough challenges. One day, not long after the enjoyable reward of staying in the luxury resort at Hayman Island, Stuart was jogging along a footpath with his trainer, an ex-international Fiji rugby player, when he fell over, suffering from what turned out to be a severe heart attack. Stuart never recovered and died as a result. He left behind a young wife and two very small children. As we gathered for his funeral, along with my former business partners, it was a very somber and uncertain future that now beckoned for many people, including me.

I was left wondering where to go from there. I had really enjoyed working as a contract coffee entrepreneur with a guy who was a big-thinking, honest, and fair but tough business entrepreneur. Who would now take his place? I felt I should step up and even though I offered to take on more responsibility, that offer was not accepted. Before long, the whole business was sold to another retail chain. They cut me back to two days per week to save money, and promoted the production manager I had been mentoring. This was disastrous for my personal family finances that had never fully recovered from the battering they had received during my negotiations with my former business partners.

I finally had to sell our home to stem the financial losses. This was absolutely devastating to me. My incredibly brave wife didn't complain or criticize me, even though she suffered as well. We had to find somewhere to rent. I couldn't face the prospect of dealing with another real estate agent asking personal questions and thankfully, a friend of my wife owned a beach holiday house nearby and kindly offered it to us at a very nominal rate.

Following is the letter of thanks I sent this generous owner a couple of years later after we had moved on:

"Thanks for letting us stay at your beach house. I want you to know what it meant to me to be able to move somewhere beautiful when I felt like a lost child of Israel, who through his own mistake was cast out and destined to wander in the wilderness. So it was for me when we were forced to sell our family home.

I am sure I suffered grief as a result of having to sell our home. Grief as a father, that I was no longer able to own and provide a home for my family. Grief that I no longer had roots in a community where I had seen my children grow up.

And yet I was so graciously offered a roof over my head by a kind and generous acquaintance. I didn't have to talk to any snotty-nosed real estate quislings, who would want to know the details of my financial agony. I just moved around the corner and over a hill to a slice of paradise. Who would have thought that so nearby there was such an idyllic place?

I loved every minute of being there. I loved coming home and soaking in the view of the wide Pacific Ocean in all its varied and tempestuous moods—an ocean that can indeed be pacific but which can also be wonderfully stormy and wild.

I loved going to sleep at night with the door ajar, and through the fly-screen, listening to the rhythm of small waves sighing and patting the shore like a friend. It is always a soothing balm for any human soul, let alone a battle-scarred and recuperating one.

I loved sitting on the balcony on any day of the week in the sun with the huge expanse of the world's biggest ocean at my side and the sun streaming on my face, giving me my dose of vitamin D like a strong, soothing medicine.

I loved coming home after a long, ferocious day at business-war in seething fractious Sydney, putting my arms in the air and drinking in the panoramic beauty and peace from the living room; saying a prayer of thanks and feeling the tension easing out of me.

I loved hearing the peculiar caw of the beachside, scrub-dwelling birds who reminded me of the only other place I could relax: our annual secret beach holiday place.

I loved how on the weekends, like a beautiful bird

showing its plumage, the ocean hosted multitudes of boats
that came out to play. Fishing boats, sailing boats, ocean-
paddling skis, leisure boats—everyone intent like me on
relaxing and soothing their battered souls.

I loved the quiet privacy of the street. It only ever
seemed to attract homely passers-by who walked their dogs
or exercised their limbs and who always seemed genial and
who, like me, must have been soaking in the regenerating
balm of the beachside air.

I loved on occasion walking down the steep bush track
to the camping ground and beach; walking along with only
a towel and book in hand, and lying in the middle of the
beach like a lone castaway on my own personal temporary
desert island.

All in all, it has been a wonderful privilege to have been
able to live in your family house at Killcare. To be able to
overlook Sydney beaches: Palm Beach, where I first met
my future wife at age seventeen; Whale Beach, where I
proposed and serenaded my fiancée at the age of twenty-two;
and in the distant view, Manly, where, as a teenager, I
surfed and grew my hair long and blond, and where we had
our first family home when the kids were small.

I know my soul has always been attracted and soothed
by the beach, and rarely has it needed it so badly or felt it so
healing as the last two and a half years that we have been so
fortunate to be able to stay at your place. And yet it is time

to move on.

There is no better place on earth that I can think of that I could have possibly wanted to be.

Thank you, with kindest regards and love from a grateful wilderness dweller."

To many in the outside world, I may have still appeared to be a successful coffee entrepreneur. But clearly, we all have our tough times. As hard as they were, I still continually tried to learn from them so as to avoid repeating any mistakes I may have made to bring these circumstances on myself, rather than blaming my circumstances or anyone else. Certainly, the biggest lesson I learned from all this was to get agreements in writing! Stuart had offered to look after me, sensing that being a contractor was not my natural station. I had become used to being the boss of my own business. He verbally offered me a future generous financial reward to provide an incentive for me to stay on with his coffee business.

Even though I had this verbal agreement with Stuart, it naturally meant nothing in the aftermath of his death and I ended up with nothing to show for our agreement. I can't blame this on anyone else. I never asked for it in writing in the first place as I trusted the man, and I am very confident that if he had not died he would have delivered on his promise. But no one else was responsible for delivering on his promise once he was no longer around.

If I had secured a written supply agreement with my former business partners between my coffee business and the main franchise business, it would have made the value of the coffee business much more clear-cut and valuable. Unfortunately, even though I asked for this a number of times, it wasn't forthcoming, and that was a calculated risk I knew I was running. Having a written agreement between Stuart and myself would have been very helpful. Who was to know that he would be run over by the proverbial 'bus' in the prime of his life? So even though you may have completely trustworthy relationships, get the agreement in writing!

I did put in place a contract with the new owners that enabled me to manage their coffee business and to supply my own customers on the side. This time, I got a good contract written by my lawyer, and got it signed. It saved me when some years later, the big company tried to lock me out of the factory. This happened as a result of a series of honest misunderstandings.

In 2008, I'd started a new business known as Espressology. This was really just a small sideline event at the time in my mind, but in spite of this the new owners saw it was growing substantially. They felt uncomfortable with this and even though we were doing a great job managing their coffee roasting and dispatch, where we were sending coffee direct to more than one thousand stores, they were looking for excuses to get me out.

One excuse they used was to suggest that one of our customers, my old friend and business partner Scott Jones, should not be able to use the facility because of a previous disaster-recovery agreement I had helped Scott establish with them. I had asked Scott to clarify the situation with them regarding using the factory so there would be no misunderstanding between them but apparently with his frantic schedule, this failed to happen. I was interstate when I got the news that padlocks had literally been put on the factory door so that neither Scott nor my team could access the factory on a Friday afternoon. This was how bad the relationship had become –they wanted an excuse to get me out. No discussion, just padlocks. My lawyer was amazed that the coffee industry seemed to attract such cowboys.

We normally did our own personal production on a Saturday so as not to interfere with the normal week's production, and this lockout would mean the end of our new business. Thankfully my lawyer talked some sense into their operations director, pointing out that any disagreements were to be in writing, according to our contract, and each respective party had thirty days to rectify the situation. Needless to say, this kind of unhealthy relationship was not a nice way to conduct business. I had been working on setting up our own new separate factory and within a few months, as my contract expired, I left them behind and started out in a new coffee-roasting facility all over again, more than thirty years after my first venture with my brother.

Along the way, as I said, I was not jealous of my former business partners' success in out-negotiating me. I wished them well. Nor was I jealous of Stuart's success, particularly since he clearly paid the ultimate price for the stress he endured. The reality was that once the lease on the little retail shop that had been dragging me down financially finally expired, I found myself practically broke. My brother-in-law Rob had lent money to the retail business as I had struggled hard to keep it afloat. The losses were only finally stemmed when my wife worked there for nothing to keep the wage costs down for the final months of the lease. The lease was in a shopping mall owned by a large corporation that sold out along the way. It was particularly onerous and is definitely the kind of situation I would avoid at all costs again. At the end of the lease, there was no option to renew and then they have you over a barrel. Either you dance to their tune or you pack up and leave.

I remember receiving a phone call at about seven p.m. one evening as I gazed out over the magnificent Pacific Ocean and Barrenjoey Lighthouse from my temporary rental house. It was a spectacular sunset and normally I wouldn't take phone calls that late, but for some reason I did. It turned out to be the leasing agent for the shop asking if we wanted another lease. I said the only way we could stay on there would be if they could reduce the rent. They refused so I said, "Okay, we will move out."

I think this leasing guy was trying too hard. In the end we did walk away with nothing but a commercial espresso machine and a couple of coffee grinders. Not long after, another café opened in this same site on a temporary cheaper lease and I found out that the young leasing agent had been fired. Apparently, the other shop owners in the mall complained because in spite of our difficulties, we were actually attracting customers to the mall and they all benefited from this. So when we closed, their sales dropped and they complained to the landlord bitterly. It was too late for us; we had moved on.

Some months prior to closing the café, however, I had rented warehouse space nearby as an office for my new bespoke contract-roasting business, Espressology, and so we could also store our furniture when we lost our home.

Apart from the little bit of exposure my wife had waiting tables in the café for a few months, she had been a stay-at-home mum for about eighteen years previous to this, doing a wonderful job raising our four kids. And before that she had been a very competent, professional hospital midwife and nurse. The only other semi-professional coffee experience she had been exposed to was serving French Press coffee in church at the end of the Sunday morning service. This however used to cause her untold stress as she worried each week about whether her roster of volunteer helpers would show up, and she also worried about any number of other tiny details. To say she wasn't very self-confident would be an understatement. And yet under the surface, I knew this other highly competent, intelligent woman. I used to be amazed at how someone who as a successful professional nurse and midwife could work so confidently, where one small mistake could result in someone actually dying, and yet she would fret over whether people got their coffee hot enough! I tried in vain many times to encourage her and 'mansplain' that no one was going to die from having to wait a little while for their free coffee to be served.

Then one fateful day, my wife came to me and asked me what I thought if she started serving coffee in the warehouse that I had recently rented for the new coffee-roasting business.

By now, we had a few decent clients on our books at Espressology and I figured if we couldn't afford the $400 per week rent on this place we may as well give up altogether. Particularly since we had three months rent-free and the first nine months at half rent on $200 per week. We had set up my home office desks and filing cabinets in this rather cavernous space, which also included most of my wife's and my personal furniture, including a ping-pong table, poker table, armchairs, sofas, and even a basketball hoop. It was basically an oversized man cave where I could smoke cigars in peace and have occasional poker nights, as well as doing some business administration from time to time. The warehouse also stored some random business equipment like barista competition stainless-steel benches.

So when my wife asked me this seemingly innocuous question about serving coffee in what was up until then my personal office and recreational space, I hesitated as I sensed that I was about to sacrifice some personal enjoyment. I agreed and said, "Okay, let's do it on a trial basis for a few months and see how it goes."

We already had the barista competition benches that could serve as kitchen benches, and we had kept the espresso machine and grinders from the store that had just closed down. So the establishment costs were just a matter of connecting the electricity and water to the machine. This only amounted to a few hundred dollars. A couple of local tradies discounted their price because they got some free coffees, did the work, and my wife didn't have to pay them right away as they were happy to be paid down the trail.

I told her that we would keep her business honest and charge her rent on the basis of 10 percent of her sales, whatever those sales happened to be. She wasn't going to get an unrealistic perception of her business viability. But within about twelve months, her 10 percent rent was more than we were paying in total rent so I handed the coffee warehouse over to her completely and Espressology set up a new factory in Sydney.

It's funny how you grow as an entrepreneur. I didn't think opening a café was that big a deal, having had a hand in opening quite a number, some obviously much more successful than others. I figured if my wife's business didn't work out it wouldn't be that much of a worry because there was so little risk. But that is not how someone just starting out for the very first time feels. My wife agonized over this humblest of low-risk, start-up businesses.

She implemented the coffee 'club' card and the free coffee-card program I had developed decades previously, and her business boomed. This success is not just because of the free coffee-card program, but more so because she is a naturally caring person, who made the business as much about loving people as it was about making a good coffee. And she naturally used the basic hospitality skills of remembering people's names and their preferences, and being genuinely interested in them.

In any case, my wife implemented the card program so that customers who were in the draw could win a prize once every month. And the prize was free coffee for a month i.e. one free cup of coffee every day for a month! To the customer the value is, say, 24 days x $4 = $96. So it's a small incentive but of value to a regular coffee drinker. The costs to the business, of course, are way less.

One particular month, the winner was a young guy who was a very smart young tradie who had a successful online business selling building products to large construction companies. He was so touched that he had won something that he very kindly bought a gas heater for the café so customers wouldn't get too cold in winter while waiting for a takeaway coffee.

Not long after this, he came to my wife and said he was thinking about opening a little café a few minutes down the road, and asked if we wouldn't mind helping him get started. He had been bitten by the coffee bug! I duly helped this enthusiastic young guy by arranging some good coffee equipment and barista training for him. He then arranged with the local authorities to convert the usage of his hired space from a general roadside store to a café, and within a short space of time, opened his doors and started serving coffee. He was no doubt a confident, take-action man.

After about six months though, he discovered that his good skill-set in getting physical structures and manual procedures sorted out quickly was one thing. Demonstrating hospitality skills and accommodating discerning coffee drinkers was quite another skill. By this time, his relationship with his girlfriend was getting strained as he juggled his two businesses and he realized that he could do much better with much less effort running his online building supply business. He then turned to me and asked if I knew anyone who might like to buy the small business.

And it was small. One of my baristas had previously asked my opinion about setting up a café in this same site and I had responded skeptically and negatively. I really didn't think at that time that this was a very viable business opportunity. Now I was being asked to re-evaluate it as a going concern, albeit a very small going concern. Its sales were only about $200 per day, which was definitely not enough to make it a viable business. But I figured if we could double the sales, it might be a viable part-time job for one person.

I thought maybe my son, Dan, might be interested. He, like many young Australians, worked as a barista after he had left school. But Dan wasn't the least bit interested in having his own coffee enterprise. Being a coffee entrepreneur is obviously not for everyone, even though Dan has used some of the same principles as I have to be a very good artistic entrepreneur.

I informed the young owner of Dan's lack of interest, and I was then asked if I knew anyone else who may want to take it off his hands, almost as if I was a business broker. Coincidentally, there was a small coffee-roasting business not far up the road that was also for sale. I figured if the two businesses could be joined together, then it might be an opportunity for a full-time job for one person. This kept me talking to the café owner and the small coffee roaster guy, both trying to sell their businesses, but it became obvious that the café owner was clearly at the end of his rope.

He told me he was going to close down and sell all the equipment online for a fraction of what he'd paid and write off the improvements he had done to the shop itself. The sale of the small coffee-roasting business fell through but by this stage, I figured that my wife and I would take the risk of buying the small café business ourselves. Once I analyzed the accounting figures a bit more, I thought maybe my wife could spread her wings and open a second store. I was confident with her newfound reputation and skills that she could attract customers and all she had to do was double the existing small sales to make it work. Even though she was reluctant, she agreed to have a go and we then arranged to pay the small amount for the equipment that I had only just recently organized for the café-owner. As a result, I knew exactly what it was worth and I negotiated to pay him over the ensuing six months. And within a few months, under my wife's charge and with her inimitable charm, elbow grease, and hospitality, the sales very quickly tripled. She had another viable new coffee business.

The local residents and holiday-makers flocked to the store. I told my wife she should get a proper lease from the property owner as the previous shop operator had only previously had an unregistered lease. This meant that if the owner sold his house, her little retail outlet would go with it and without a registered lease, the new owners could take over the now viable store themselves and all my wife's hard work would be for nothing. I organized for my lawyer to draw up a proper lease and the owner agreed to meet with my wife to sign it.

On the day the signing was due to take place, the owner didn't show up. Within a few days, we saw him guiding some prospective buyers through the property. All my worst fears seemed to be materializing. But my wife, with clear feminine wisdom, asked the owner what he wanted for the property. It turned out that the offer he had received was about $20,000 less than his desired amount. My wife told him she would see what she could do to get the amount needed.

She then spoke to her long-suffering father who agreed to lend us the 10 percent deposit because we still had no savings or capital. He very generously agreed because he could see the deep desire his daughter had for her own maternal nest for children and hopefully future grandchildren. The owner agreed to sell his property to us. We then engaged a mortgage broker who understood the bank bureaucracy, as it would no doubt be very difficult to find a lender who would agree to a mortgage for a couple in their late fifties and who were more likely to be near retirement with no long-standing earning capacity.

I had calculated that with the additional rent from the shop and a separate self-contained cabin that came with the house, our mortgage repayments would actually be slightly less than the rent we were paying for our current house. It was a great and rare opportunity.

The mortgage broker very skillfully navigated the banking labyrinth and found a bank who would lend the money to us. But once the application went in, the bank came back and informed us that because of the little roadside shop out the front of the house, the entire property was classified as commercial, and commercial properties require a 20 percent deposit, not 10 percent.

My poor wife was devastated. After all her hard work and effort, and thinking she might once again have her own house, we were blocked at the final hurdle. The next morning, which happened to be a Sunday, my wife was lying in bed late feeling extremely depressed. I was preparing some toast and a cup of tea to try and cheer her up when a knock came from the front door of the house we were renting.

It was a neighbor who was also a customer at the our new local café. It was a bit of a shock to have someone randomly knocking on our door so early on a Sunday morning, let alone someone we didn't really know that well. He was a very cheery intelligent man and so I invited him in for a cup of tea, while my wife was embarrassed because she was still dressed in her nightie and in bed.

As soon as he walked in, I just heard the words in my head: "Tell him, tell him, tell him." I thought that was a bit weird but sure enough, the conversation soon came around to what we were up to. I humbled myself and told him, "The bank has knocked back our loan application unless we can come up with the extra 10 percent for the deposit."

He immediately asked, "How much is the extra 10 percent?"

I replied, "It's eighty-three thousand dollars."

Without hesitation, he said, "No worries. I will go and write a check for you and I'll be back in a few hours' time."

My wife and I looked at each other in bewilderment. Sure enough, a few hours later this incredible man walked back in our front door with a check rounded up and made out to us for $85,000. As he handed it over to me, he said, "I don't want you to pay any interest and pay it back when you can."

I said, "It might be a couple of years before we can repay you."

"No worries," he said. "We'll just write a simple agreement between ourselves in case I die so my children know what I have done with some of their inheritance." And with that, he walked out again.

The following Monday morning, bright and early, we told the mortgage broker we had a 20 percent deposit for the bank. The bank in due course lent us the money and we had a new mortgage and a new house. The reality was that we had no real equity. We had no idea how we were going to pay this lovely man back, let alone my wife's father. I had been steadily paying my brother-in-law back each month but I still owed him money too.

About two and a half years later, a real estate agent dropped a leaflet in our letterbox showing valuations of properties that had recently sold in our area and an estimated valuation of our property. I was shocked. It appeared that our house had increased by over 50 percent, and this was at the lower end of their estimated value.

I immediately took the leaflet to a local competitor bank and asked them if they would be interested in re-mortgaging our house based on the new valuation. The said yes! To cut a long story short, we got a new mortgage that enabled me to pay off our very kind neighbor, my wife's father, my brother-in-law, and $50,000 of credit card debt all in one go. This was only a few short months ago. I spent the entire month walking around feeling like a huge weight had been lifted off my shoulders. It had been almost fourteen long, hard years trudging through a very dark valley.

I finally felt like I had turned a corner at the ripe old age of sixty. And this was all because my wife obeyed that still small voice and started serving coffee in an obscure warehouse, and because she'd offered something for free to be generous to her customers. It was also because I obeyed my conscience and humbled myself to reveal my vulnerability in telling an acquaintance about our dire financial situation.

We had drifted from rental home to rental home, and I'd become used to the feeling of being adrift, and kind of enjoyed the lack of responsibility. I didn't of course realize at the time how deeply depressed I was. This was a fourteen-year grinding trial from the time I first started negotiating with my former business partners until I finally paid off the huge personal debt that I had accrued.

That was one very tough season.

After having been forced to sell our home some seven years previously and being technically bankrupt, all this new found blessing had come from the small free coffee card! Herein lies the story. How to go from being regarded internationally as a successful coffee entrepreneur to being technically bankrupt and back again.

My wife's hard work and courage played a major part in being freed from debt to friends and family. True are the words from the ancient proverb: "She looks well to the ways of her household and does not eat the bread of idleness. Her children rise up and call her blessed; her husband also, and he praises her: 'Many women have done excellently but you surpass them all.'"

One of the earliest memories that I can claim as my own, one that was not just a story about me repeated to me by adults around me as I was growing up, was finally confirmed as I entered my seventh decade on this planet. The simple song I was taught in Sunday school as a three-year-old, "The Wise Man Built His House Upon the Rock", has come back to me as possibly the most important lesson we can learn as human beings. To be wise, we need to put into action what our good conscience prompts us to do or say. The moral of the parable is that while both men hear God's voice, only the wise man acts on the basis of it. The foolish man who builds his house on the sand, doesn't act on it. We obviously all stumble, make mistakes, and get off track. We do things that we regret and are sorry for, but in the end, all we can do is pay attention to that still, small voice and keep taking obedient steps in our own personal thousand-mile journey.

Lesson 20

LISTEN
TO YOUR
CONSCIENCE

My plan now is to transition to retirement from my current business over the next few years, but even as I write, I feel I am being nudged towards yet another new business opportunity. It may mean yet again leaving the ease and comfort of familiar surroundings, and striking out into more uncertain and unknown places and risking the future. This is the nature of life, and it is the nature of being an entrepreneur. An Australian coffee entrepreneur.

As the ancient proverb says, "A man's mind plans his way, but God directs his steps"—even in Australia.

The End …
… of the beginning.

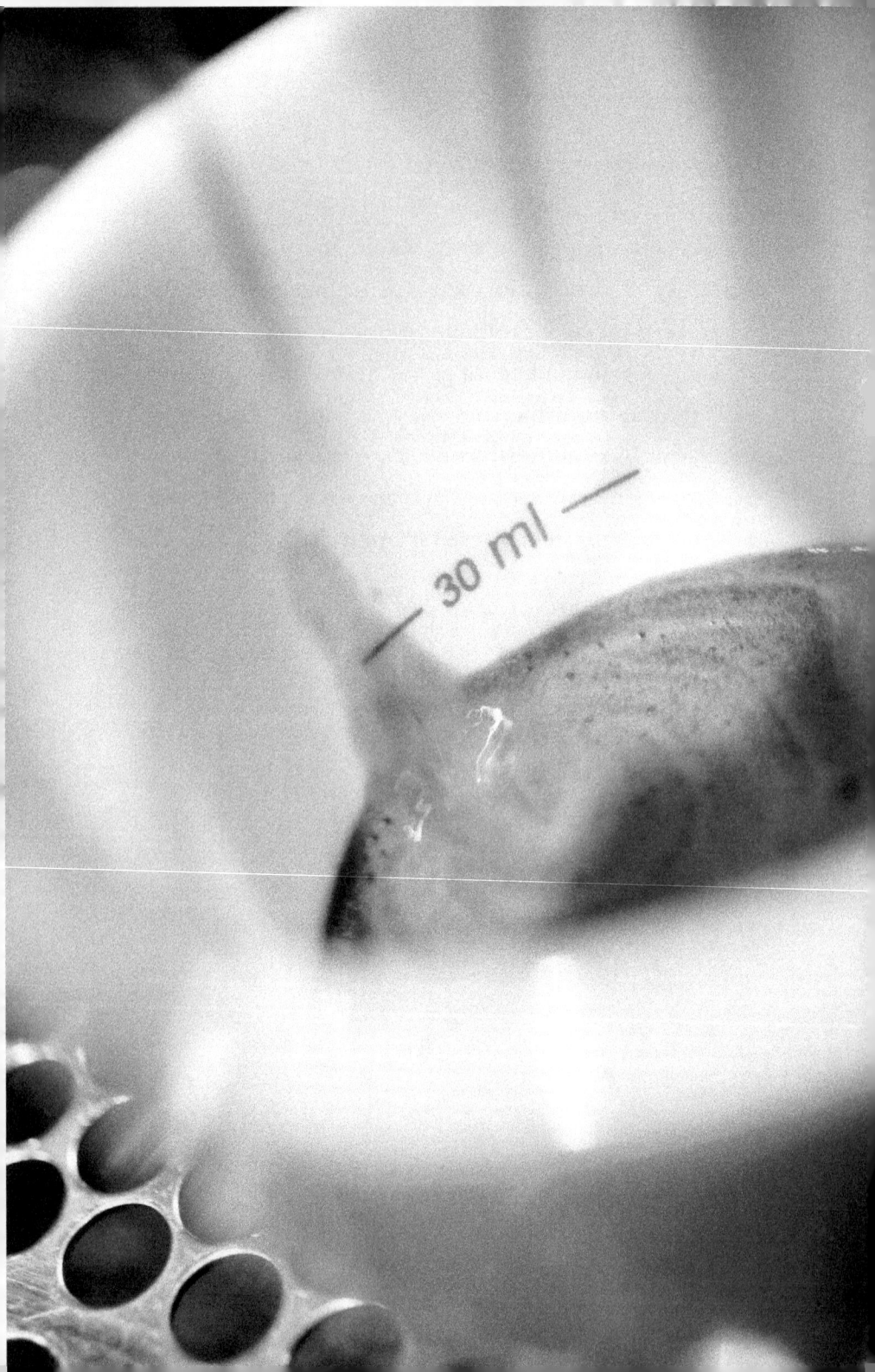

CPSIA information can be obtained
at www.ICGtesting.com
Printed in the USA
BVHW041802110920
588613BV00011B/1048